PLANTS OF
BIG BASIN REDWOODS
STATE PARK

PLANTS OF BIG BASIN REDWOODS STATE PARK
and the Coastal Mountains of Northern California

Mary Beth Cooney-Lazaneo
Kathleen Lyons

Photography by Howard King

Mountain Press Publishing Company
Missoula, 1981

Pen and ink illustrations by Emily Silver

Library of Congress Cataloging in Publication Data

Cooney-Lazaneo, Mary Beth.
    Plants of Big Basin Redwoods State Park and the
coastal mountains of northern California.

    1. Botany—California—Big Basin Redwoods
State Park. 2. Botany—California—Coast Range.
3. Plants, Useful—California—Big Basin Redwoods
State Park—Identification. 4. Plants, Useful—
California—Santa Cruz Mountains—Identification.
5. Big Basin Redwoods State Park, Calif.
6. Coast Range, Calif. I. Lyons, Kathleen,
joint author. II. Title.
QK149.C64   582.13'09794'71   80-16687
ISBN 0-87842-135-1

Acknowledgments

We greatly appreciate the support and encouragement from the many people who helped make this book possible: Howard King, for his stunning photographs and never-ending enthusiasm and patience in both the woods and the darkroom; Barb Danforth, for her review of the manuscript, her companionship along many of the trails, and her preliminary plant sketches; Dr. William Doyle, professor at the University of California at Santa Cruz, for much of our original guidance; Ron Irvin, former Big Basin Docent Chairman, for the use of his beautiful pictures in the unpublished form of the book; Jim and Juanita Cooney for their help on hiking, typing, and pulling this book together; and to the many friendly rangers and park staff at Big Basin Redwoods State Park. We would also like to give special thanks to Tony Look and the Sempervirens Fund for their strong moral support, and for, beyond helping us, having done so much to preserve the beauty of the Santa Cruz Mountains.

Also, we are deeply grateful for the constant assistance and patience of Neil and Marge Lyons, Andy Lazaneo, John Stanley, and Janeane Wilkey.

METRIC SYSTEM TABLE

1 mm. = approx. 1/25 of an inch
10 mm. = 1 cm. (approx. 2/5 of an inch)
10 cm. =   1 dm. (approx. 4 inches)
10 dm. = 1 m. (approx. 40 inches)

Contents

San Lorenzo Valley and the Santa Cruz Mountains

Introduction

This book is designed for hikers and nature lovers who are interested in the plants around them, but have little or no botanical experience. Each plant has a color photograph and a short non-technical description, which includes general localities where the plant can be found and some interesting historical and cultural information. In the few places where specialized botanical vocabulary was necessary for accuracy the terms are explained in the Glossary. Associated with the Glossary are drawings of flower parts and other plant structures.

Although the field work for this book was done mostly in the Santa Cruz Mountains and especially in Big Basin Redwoods State Park, the majority of these plants grow throughout the coastal mountains, extending north through the redwood region to the Oregon border.

This broad range of mountainous country contains a great diversity of plant and animal communities. Many of these habitats merge with others to at least some extent so there is no standard group of communities agreed upon by all botanists. For simplicity, we have listed only the most basic communities.

Probably the best-known habitat is the redwood forest. Coast redwoods form almost pure stands with only occasional Douglas fir, tan oak, madrone, and bay trees intermingled. Here a moist, shady forest floor combined with thick, acidic redwood duff accumulated over the years limits the number of species. Shrubs, such as huckleberry, western azalea, and California rhododendron can tolerate this shade and sometimes create dense thickets. Streams in the redwood communities often have lush growth but are so dominated by the towering redwoods that they are not considered true riparian or streamside habitats.

Mixed evergreen forests are often found on drier slopes above the redwood communities. Here Douglas fir and tan oak are abundant, with smaller concentrations of oak, madrone, bay, wax myrtle, hazel, and redwood. Since these forests are much more open, allowing more light penetration, many species of plants grow abundantly on the floor. Most plants in this book can be found here.

Oak woodland communities grow along many of the dry upper ridges. These forests, comprised of coast live, canyon, interior live, or black oak, are extremely open, with large, sunny patches of grasses and flowers scattered between the trees.

On the hottest, driest, southwest-facing slopes are the dense impenetrable thickets of the chaparral community. The plants in these regions survive extremely harsh environmental conditions and have developed several common adaptations. Most plants here are evergreen with small, light-colored, moisture-conserving leaves. Often these leaves are covered with small hairs or a waxy coating as further protection from moisture loss. Most of these plants are also well adapted to frequent fires. The most common plants in this community are manzanita, chamise, yerba santa, sage, and buckbrush. Knobcone pine is sometimes included as a member of the chaparral and sometimes as a separate community.

At the opposite end of the environmental scene is the riparian or streamside community. Plants of this habitat are not only assured a constant water supply, but are often flooded in winter. Sycamore, maple, box elder, and cottonwood dominate the vegetation in this well-watered setting.

Guidelines For Using This Book

For quick identification of plants, this book is arranged in four major categories: conifers, broadleaf trees, flowers, and ferns. Conifer trees are those which bear their seeds in cones; they are usually evergreen and have needle-like leaves. Broadleaf trees reproduce by flowers, some so small that they are unnoticeable on casual observation. Their broad, flat green leaves can be evergreen or deciduous.

The flower section of this book includes both shrubs and herbaceous (non-woody) plants. For easy identification these plants are broken down into several color groups: pink-red, blue-purple, green-white, and yellow-orange. However, these colors are not absolute and in some cases more than one color group should be checked. For example, some plants have shades ranging from pale pink to purple depending on the individual plant and its stage of maturity. A few plants range drastically from white to purple as they mature. Still others have similar quantities of two different colors and their placement in the book is rather arbitrary.

The last section of the book contains ferns and fern allies. These are herbaceous plants which reproduce by spores.

Each plant has its scientific name listed as well as its common name. Unlike common names, which vary from region to region and even person to person, the scientific names are universally accepted terms, with only one official name per plant. The first word, the genus name, is capitalized and may be shared by many similar species. The second part, in lower case, is the specific name, which belongs only to that particular species. Both of these names are always underlined or italicized. Occasionally, varieties are acknowledged within a certain species. Also included are the common and scientific family names; a family is composed of several different genera. In addition, the most common blooming period for each flowering plant is listed.

We would like to remind the reader that although many uses are listed, it is illegal to pick anything from State Park lands. Without this law, many of our beautiful plants would no longer be here for us to enjoy and certainly would not be present for future generations. Some of these plants are so rare or so beautiful that they shouldn't be picked anywhere.

Many plants are forage for native wildlife and the animals of this area have plenty of natural food available to them. Do not feed the animals; human handouts are detrimental to their health.

Local Conservation Organizations

We hope this book increases your enjoyment and awareness of these exceptional mountains. Should you be interested in learning more about them, or taking an active part in their preservation there are several fine organizations which are dedicated to these goals. The Sempervirens Fund is a conservation organization which raises funds for the enlargement of Santa Cruz Mountain State Parks and their trail networks. The Santa Cruz Mountain Trail Association promotes recreational uses within the parks and sponsors several trail maintenance projects. The California Native Plant Society promotes preservation of the native flora. Other organizations which are active include the Save-the-Redwoods League, the Santa Cruz Mountains Natural History Association, and local chapters of the Sierra Club and National Audobon Society.

Conifers

Santa Cruz Cypress

Cypress Family
Cupressaceae Family

Cupressus abramsiana

The Santa Cruz cypress is a rare and endangered tree of the Santa Cruz Mountains. Found in only a few locations, it inhabits dry, often sterile, inland marine sand deposits and sandstone outcroppings. Unfortunately, due to increased development within this unique environment, the cypress is threatened with extinction.

Related to many cultivated varieties of cypress, this native grows to heights of 50 to 60 feet and has thick bright green foliage. Small overlapping scale-like leaves grow along the branches. The cones, found at the tips of these branches, are closed until the second season and upon maturity release tiny, brown, winged seeds.

California Nutmeg

Yew Family
Taxaceae Family

Torreya californica

The California nutmeg, also known as the torrey pine, grows in many habitats throughout the Santa Cruz Mountains and north along the Coast Range, but is not particularly common in any. One of the largest Torrey pines in these mountains grows at Camp Herbert along Waddell Creek in Big Basin State Park.

Although the California nutmeg is most often seen in a shrub-like form, it occasionally grows forty or more feet tall. Lying flat off the branches, the needles are a glossy green with sharp pointed tips. The large fruit formed after pollination of the female ovules hangs from the outer branches, changing from olive green to a deep purple as it ripens. A large seed inside somewhat resembles commercial nutmeg, but is not related.

Early Indian tribes used the root of the California nutmeg for a basketry thread. The sharp needle tips were also used as instruments for tatooing.

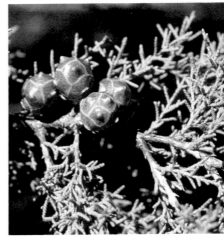

Santa Cruz Cypress

California Nutmeg

Douglas Fir

Pseudotsuga menziesii

The Douglas fir is one of the most common trees in the mixed evergreen forest, and is a prominent member of the redwood forest.

Besides being one of the most common trees, this native is one of the largest, second in size only to the coast redwoods. Because of their size, Douglas firs are sometimes confused with redwoods, but there are many distinguishing features between the two trees, the most outstanding being the bark. Both trees have furrowed bark, but the redwoods have long deep parallel grooves running the entire length of the tree, while Douglas-fir grooves are short and not so symmetrically parallel. The bark of Douglas fir is a dark gray, while redwood bark is a deep reddish brown. The light green single needles grow in whorls around drooping stems. Although these stems droop, the sharply uplifted branches give the tree an erect profile. The cones, which mature in one year, hang from the branch tips. These cones are 3 to 4 inches long and have 3-forked bracts between the rounded scales.

Douglas fir had many uses in the past, and is still important today. Medicinally it was used as a treatment for rheumatism and tuberculosis. For rheumatism, Indians covered boughs with soil and burned them in the steamhouse while the patient lay on a blanket above. A tea, high in vitamin C, was brewed from the needles to treat lung troubles and tuberculosis

Smoke from burning limbs was used as a good luck charm. It was believed that by holding their bows over the smoke, hunters would be undetectable to deer, and the hunt would be successful. Another hunting use involved fashioning a shaft from the branches, which was used as a salmon spear.

In basketry, the long thin roots were separated and used for thread. Today Douglas fir is an important tree to the lumber industry, and is the most important lumber tree from California to British Columbia.

Douglas Fir

Knobcone Pine

Pine Family
Pinaceae Family

Pinus attenuata

The knobcone pine is native to California and can be found on dry slopes, often where few other trees can survive. This adaptation to poor soil conditions makes it a hardy pioneer plant for recently burned or disturbed areas. It is found on the upper ridges in Big Basin, Castle Rock, Butano, and Henry Cowell State Parks.

Because of its harsh environment, the knobcone pine is usually sparce and scraggly. The needles, which grow in clusters of 3 on slender branches, range from 4 to 7 inches in length. Closed woody cones adhere tightly to the trunk and branches, opening only in extreme heat to release the small seeds.

Like most other pines, the seeds are edible either raw or roasted. They can be gathered by heating the cones until the bracts open, allowing the seeds to fall out.

Knobcone Pine

Coast Redwood

Redwood Family
Taxodiaceae Family

Sequoia sempervirens

The coast redwood is the most outstanding tree in this area, and because of its immense size and beauty, it was instrumental to the establishment of Big Basin Redwoods State Park in the early 1900s. Today the redwood dominates most of the shaded valleys, mixing with Douglas-fir on drier slopes and upper canyons.

Often reaching a height of 300 to 350 feet and a diameter of 12 to 16 feet, the coast redwood is the largest tree in these mountains. The thick bark, with its deep furrows running the length of the tree, is a rich reddish brown. It is this bark that gives the Redwood its excellent fire resistant quality. The dark green leaves are needle-like and grow flat off the branches. Small cones, usually about an inch long, hang from the branch tips, releasing tiny brown seeds when mature. Of these seeds, only 15 to 20 percent germinate and grow into seedlings. Redwoods are also capable of sprouting from the roots of parent trees. These sprouts, because of already established root systems, grow more vigorously than seedlings and so are the more common form of reproduction.

Coastal Indians were the first to make use of the stately redwood. The strong roots were dug up, stripped for their fibers, and used as a thread in baskets. Today, the coast redwood is primarily used for lumber.

**Coast
Redwood**

Broadleaf Trees

California Hazel

Hazel Family
Corylaceae Family

Corylus californica
Blooms: (females) January-March

California hazel is a common shrub of shaded areas within the Coast Range. It can be found on wooded slopes as well as near streams and creeks.

Reaching 3 to 10 feet in height, these large shrubs have smooth slender stems and an open, spreading appearance. The alternate leaves have rounded bases and sharply pointed tips. Their softness and fine double-toothed margins are characteristic features. In October and November, slender, 1 to 3 inch long catkins appear and release pollen from January to March. In late spring and summer the nuts mature, covered by a tubular, bristly husk.

These nuts are not only edible, but are comparable in flavor to commercial filberts. They can also be ground into a meal and baked into bread.

Stems from this shrub were useful in basketry. To prepare the stems for weaving, the Indians either scraped them with a sharp rock or peeled the bark off with their teeth. After this procedure the lightweight stems were used as thread, rimhoops, or foundations for baskets, some as fine as flour seives.

California Hazel

California Box Elder

Maple Family
Aceraceae Family

Acer negundo var. *californicum*
Blooms: March-April

Box elder grows along the banks of streams. Although not commonly seen in all areas, it is especially abundant along the San Lorenzo River.

Reaching 30 or more feet in height, this tree has opposite compound leaves that hang on long slender stems. Each leaf is composed of 3 leaflets that are lobed and have toothed margins. In spring, small male and female flowers appear on separate trees. The male flowers hang on small thin stems, profusely covering the trees. Winged seeds called samaras are red when young, turning a golden straw color with age.

Blue Elderberry

Honeysuckle Family
Caprifoliaceae Family

Sambucus mexicana

Coast Red Elderberry

Sambucus callicarpa
Blooms: March-June

Two species of elderberries are commonly found in these mountains, growing in extremely different habitats. Coast red elderberry grows near the coast in moist shaded valleys. It is especially common along the streams in Butano State Park. Blue elderberry, on the other hand, prefers dry slopes in the chaparral regions.

Both plants are characterized by the same distinct leaf pattern. The leaves are compound with 6 to 8 finely toothed leaflets in an opposite pattern along the stem, ending in a final leaflet at the tip. In spring small, white, star-shaped flowers are borne in clusters 6 to 10 inches wide. Blue elderberry clusters are flat-topped and ripen into deep blue berries, while the red elderberry has dome-shaped clusters which ripen to scarlet red.

The light stems had several uses. Indians cut the plants back each fall so that in spring the shoots would be straight enough to make arrows. Children hollowed out the pithy stems to make flutes and peashooters. Indians of Southern California also used the berry stems to make a blackish dye for their basketry designs.

Although the blue berries are edible when cooked, most if not all of the red berries are poisonous.

California Box Elder

Blue Elderberry
Blue Elderberry

California Bay

Umbellularia californica
Blooms: December-April

California bay grows on wooded slopes of the Santa Cruz Mountains. Although common in most area parks, it is seldom seen in Big Basin. Only a few trees are present along Sunset and Berry Creek Trails.

The leaves, which are wedge shaped at the base and pointed at the tips, somewhat resemble wax myrtle leaves, but can be distinguished by their pungent fragrance. Arranged in an alternate pattern, these leaves are leatherly and usually dark green. In early spring small yellowish-green flowers develop and profusely cover the tree.

The bay tree had many uses for the Indians, the most important being medicinal. Leaves were used to cleanse wounds and to cure headaches. For headaches the leaves were either bound around the head or placed up the nostril. Leaves steeped in boiling water were used as a disinfectant, while smoke from leaves burned directly on the fire was used as a "vaporizer" for colds. For treatment of rheumatism the Indians would rub their bodies with bay oil while taking their steambaths. The combination of the stinging bay oil and a complete body rubdown was supposed to be an effective cure. Evidently there was some merit to this since the settlers later adopted the treatment. However, instead of using it in steambaths, they mixed the oil with lard and covered their bodies with liniment.

Bay nuts were roasted and later eaten whole, or ground into flour and baked into breads. Roasting removed the bitter taste caused by the high acid content.

A more curious use for the leaves was as a flea repellent in Indian dwellings. By spreading leaves on the floor they kept their living quarters flea free.

Today the bay is still useful. Leaves are dried and ground into a spice which is similar to the expensive European bay leaves. The wood, which is white and fine-grained, is used under the name of Oregon myrtle to make bowls and other ornamental objects.

Black Cottonwood

Populus trichocarpa
Blooms: February-April

Black cottonwood is found in riparian communities. A large number grow along the banks of the San Lorenzo River.

Commonly reaching heights of 75 feet or more, the cottonwood tree is known by its gray striated bark. Smooth green spear-shaped leaves hang from the branches on long stems. In early spring, male and female flowers, arranged in catkins, hang from the branches.

Both the catkins and inner bark of cottonwood are edible, either raw or boiled.

California Bay

Black Cottonwood

California Buckeye

Aesculus californica
Blooms: April-June

The habitat of California buckeye ranges from open dry slopes to wooded canyons. It is farily abundant throughout the Santa Cruz Mountains and along the northern Coast Range.

In late spring this is one of the showiest natives in this area. Fresh bright green leaves have replaced the bare limbs of winter. Characteristically, the leaves are palmate and composed of 5 to 7 leaflets. Large fragrant white flower spikes also begin to appear. By the end of summer, the leaves have fallen and the flowers replaced by large brown chestnut-like fruits.

Inedible before leaching, the toxic nuts were used in the capture of fish by California Indians. Mashed nuts floated on the surface of the water acted to stupify the fish, enabling them to be more easily caught.

After leaching, the starchy nuts were ground into a paste which was eaten cold or baked into bread. Two common methods of leaching were used. The nuts were either steamed in a fire pit for several hours, sliced, and placed in water for 2 to 5 days, or they were steamed, peeled and mashed, then soaked in water for approximately one hour.

Golden Chinquapin

Castanopsis chrysophylla
Blooms: July-August

Golden chinquapin grows in dry woods and chaparral areas within the Coast Range.

The leaves of the chinquapin are tapered at both the base and tip, somewhat resembling California bay leaves. Like many chaparral plants, these leaves have a thick, leathery texture. A covering of small golden hairs on the underside of the leaf gives the golden chinquapin its name. The female flowers appear in late summer, are pollinated by male catkins, and produce clustered nuts in September. Each nut is surrounded with spiny bracts which give it the appearance of a large burr.

These sweet-tasting nuts can be roasted and eaten much like the chestnut. They are also a favorite of squirrels and other small animals who gather the nuts for their winter food supply.

California Buckeye

Golden Chinquapin

California Buckeye

Madrone

Arbutus menziesii
Blooms: March-May

Madrone is one of the most common trees in the Santa Cruz Mountains. Although only occasionally found in the deeper redwood valleys, it is quite common on the upper slopes and ridges where it often forms dense stands.

Because of its constant search for light, this large native tree often assumes unusual gnarled and twisted shapes. Another unusual feature of the tree is the characteristic thin bark on the trunks and limbs. Each summer much of this outer bark peels off and hangs in tatters, exposing smooth light green wood which weathers to a rich red brown. The evergreen leaves are a waxy green and grow alternately along the branches. In early spring small clusters of waxy, white, bell-shaped flowers appear, and in late summer these mature into large orange berries.

This tree was used for food, medicine, and utensils by both Indians and settlers. Roots and leaves were brewed into a tea to treat stomachaches. Sores and wounds were treated with a lotion made from the leaves and bark. Whether eaten raw or boiled in baskets with hot rocks, the berries were an important food. When dried they were stored and used as an important winter staple.

The fine-grained wood of the madrone was used by Indians for lodgepoles and by some early settlers to make stirrups. Charcoal from the burned wood reportedly made an excellent gunpowder, which was sold commercially.

Madrone

Red Alder

Alnus oregona
Blooms: (female) January-March

Red alder can be found in moist areas throughout the Santa Cruz Mountains.

This native tree can be recognized by its gray-white patchy bark and coarsely toothed alternate leaves. Although similar to the white alder in appearance, the leaf edges of red alder curl under while the leaf edges of white alder do not. In February and March, long male catkins release pollen which fertilizes the cone-like female catkins. By autumn, the seeds are ripe and are shed from the cone as winged nutlets.

The main use for red alder by California Indians was in basketry. Roots were used for weaving thread, while the inner bark produced an orange dye. Chunks of the bark were cooked until soft, chewed until the dye was released, then spit into a stone dish. The acid in the saliva set the color, which turned to a rich brown with age.

Big Leaved Maple

Acer macrophyllum
Blooms: March-May

This large native tree is usually found in moist areas or along streams. A particularly nice stand grows near the old lime kilns in Fall Creek State Park.

When the maple is young it has smooth light gray bark, but as it grows older it becomes darker gray-brown with large cracks and ridges. At maturity the tree can reach up to 80 feet in height. Its large 3 to 5-lobed palmate leaves turn bright yellow or orange in the fall. Before new leaves grow again in spring, long drooping clusters of yellowish-green flowers appear. These flowers ripen into double winged fruits, called samaras, which blow easily in the wind.

Although this maple is not widely used, its sap can be made into syrup.

Several other parts of the tree were used as basket materials. Sapwood was used as thread, bark as a rim blinding, and stem as a warp.

Red Alder **Big Leaved Maple**

Big Leaved Maple

Oaks

Quercus species

Although oaks have variable forms, they have several common characteristics. Ripening from the female flowers are the acorns, which are composed of a smooth, thin-shelled nut protruding from a scaly cap. The male flowers hang down in pendant catkins.

Since these trees have similar cultural uses, they are included under one heading with separate descriptions for individual species.

Uses:

The oaks were one of the most important food sources of the California Indians. Acorns were gathered by the women and thrown over their backs into large baskets, called burden baskets. Older women didn't join in the gathering, but instead enjoyed the privilege of sorting the wormy acorns from the whole ones. After years of eating acorns containing grit from leaching and grinding with rocks, these women had only stubby remnants of teeth. Therefore, the soft worms from the "bad" acorns were considered a great delicacy. This privilege of the old served a two-fold purpose, since it also kept worms from laying eggs in the acorns and destroying the meat before it could be used. After sorting, the acorns were soaked overnight in hot water, hulled, and ground into meal. Since acorns contain a bitter tannic acid, they had to go through a complicated process of leaching before being eaten. This was usually done either by placing the meal in a frame of twigs and letting water run over it, or by boiling it by the hot rock method. In this process the meal was placed in watertight baskets and hot rocks from the fire were added until the water boiled. Since the water had to be changed several times to remove the dissolved tannic acid this was a tedious process. After leaching, the meal was made into a thin gruel or wrapped in fern leaves and baked on hot rocks.

Acorns were important medicinally as well. Before it had been discovered by modern civilization, a type of penicillin was used by the Indians to draw out sores and boils. The acorn meal was covered tightly to cause mold to form, then, when this layer of mold or "skin" was strong enough to be pulled off, it was rolled into sheets and stored until needed.

The wood from some of our local oaks has been important in the past, and some is still used today. Although the spreading form of the coastal live oak precludes its use for lumber, the wood burns well and is often used as a fuel and a source of charcoal. The maul oak (canyon oak) received its name because its wood is so hard and heavy that it was used to make maul heads in the pioneer days.

Coast Live Oak

Quercus agrifolia
Blooms: February-April

The Coast Live Oak is the most common oak in these mountains, inhabiting mixed evergreen forests, oak woodlands, and grasslands.

When uncrowded by other trees, this oak develops a distinctive rounded crown with wide spreading branches. The sharply-toothed leaves have a shiny dark green upper surface, and a lower surface covered with tufts of tan fuzz. Sometimes mistaken for the interior live oak, the coast live oak has deep curved-under leaves. Oblong acorns grow from a fringed cap and end in a pointed tip.

California Black Oak

Quercus kelloggii
Blooms: March-May

Growing in open oak woodlands, black oaks are most often seen at higher elevations on the eastern slopes of the mountains. Several large groves are present at Castle Rock State Park.

Unlike most other oaks, the black oak is deciduous. When the leaves first appear in spring they are red and covered with fine hairs. Later they mature to deep green. Like those of the white oak *(Quercus lobata)*, which grows in the interior valleys, these leaves are deeply lobed. However, they can be distinguished by the spiny points on the lobe margins.

Coast Live Oak

Coast Live Oak

California Black Oak

Interior Live Oak

Quercus wislizeni
Blooms: April-Mary

This medium-sized oak inhabits dry wooded slopes, often mixing and hybridizing with the coast live oak.

The glossy green leaves of the interior live oak are leathery with sharply-toothed margins. They differ from the coast live oak in that they are relatively flat and lack the short fuzz on the under surface. Like canyon oak, the slender acorns mature and drop in their second autumn.

Canyon Oak

Quercus chrysolepis
Blooms: May-June

The canyon or maul oak, like most oaks, is found on dry wooded slopes of the Coast Range.

Largest of the western oaks, this oak has been known to grow to a diameter of ten feet. The leaves have variable margins, ranking from smooth to coarsely toothed, often on the same twig. They are usually characterized by a golden fuzz on the underside, and a glossy green upper surface. In autumn, the second year acorns with the golden-tinged, rounded caps, fall to the ground.

Scrub Oak

Quercus dumosa
Blooms: April-June

Scrub oak grows in dry chaparral regions throughout the Coastal Mountains.

Due to the harsh conditions in which it is found, this oak grows as a shrub. The glossy green leaves are small, thick, and leathery.

Interior Live Oak
Canyon Oak

Western Sycamore

Sycamore Family
Platanaceae Family

Platanus racemosa
Blooms: March-April

The western sycamore grows along river banks throughout the Central Coast Mountains. It is especially common along the San Lorenzo River, often forming large groves.

Reaching heights of up to 100 feet, this tree has smooth, thin, whitish bark, arranged in jigsaw-like pieces. The sharp contrast of the white tree trunk with the surrounding vegetation makes it a striking tree. The palmate leaves of the Sycamore are light green and deeply lobed. Small hairs cover both surfaces, giving them a velvety texture. Small clusters of flowers hang from the stems in spring, later ripening into round fruits which remain on the tree throughout winter, then break open to release small winged seeds.

The wood of the sycamore is strong, fine-grained and hard to split; it is only used as a fuel source.

Western Sycamore

California Wax Myrtle

Myrica californica
Blooms: April-June

Wax myrtle is found scattered throughout mixed evergreen and redwood forests.

Growing as a large shrub or small tree, depending on its environment, myrtle is sometimes confused with California bay because of similar leaves. Like the bay, the leaves are long, slender, and dark green, but they differ in that they are slightly serrated and somewhat broader at the tip. Also, they lack the pungent smell of bay. The short male catkins are borne on lower leaf axils, while the longer female catkins are borne on upper axils. Berries, produced by the female catkins, are greenish purple with a waxy white covering.

Although there is no reference to the western myrtles being used this way, the waxy berries of an Atlantic species are used to make candles. First they're boiled, then set aside to cool. Gradually the wax which coats them rises to the top where it can then be scraped off and made into naturally-scented candles.

Tan Oak

Lithocarpus densiflora
Blooms: May-July

The tan oak is a common resident of the mixed evergreen forest and can be found on most forested trails in these mountains.

This tree, which is not a true oak, grows straight and tall and has smooth gray bark. Its glossy green leaves are brittle and coarsely toothed along the margins. In late spring erect clusters of flowers appear, which mature into acorns after two years. These differ from true oak acorns by the bristly appearance of the cap.

Tan oak acorns were prepared like oak acorns for food and medicine (see oaks). Tannic acid, used to tan leather, is derived from these trees. At one time Big Basin State Park was an important source of tan oaks. Large sections of bark were stripped from the trees, dried, and shipped to Santa Cruz by wagon. There they were boiled to leach the acid from the bark.

California Wax Myrtle

Tan Oak

Flowers — Pink to Red

Western Burning Bush

Staff Tree Family
Celastraceae Family

Euonymus occidentalis
Blooms: April-July

Western burning bush is found near streams in the mixed evergreen and redwood forests. Although not commonly seen along most Santa Cruz Mountain creeks, it is fairly abundant along upper Berry Creek in Big Basin State Park and Little Butano Creek in Butano State Park.

An unusual leaf pattern easily distinguishes this large bush. The dark green leaves are arranged oppositely along the stem, with the last pair forming a distinctive fork. Brownish-red flowers, which ripen into deep red berries in late summer, hang on small stalks beneath the leaf junctions.

Another name for this shrub is pawnbroker's bush because the fruits hang down in clusters of three resembling the pawn shop symbol.

Canyon Gooseberry

Gooseberry Family
Grossulariaceae Family

Grossularia leptosma
Blooms: March-June

Gooseberry grows in shady wooded areas, especially alongside creeks. It is particularly abundant along Little Butano Creek in Butano State Park.

Red spines cover the stems and berries of this shrub. Its palmate leaves are alternately arranged. Fuschia-like in appearance, the small hanging flowers are red at the base with white petals.

All species in the genus have edible berries, high in vitamin C, which were eaten raw, or cooked in pies, preserves, and jellies. Also, like currants, the berries were dried, mixed with animal fat, and eaten while traveling.

Western Burning Bush

**Western
Burning
Bush**

Canyon Gooseberry

Lovely Clarkia

Clarkia `concinna

Large Godetia

Clarkia purpurea
Blooms: April-August

Clarkia is found on dry grassy or brushy slopes throughout the Coastal Range. In early summer, these colorful wildflowers make attractive displays on the hillsides.

Growing along tall graceful stems, both lovely Clarkia and large Godetia have small alternate linear leaves. The narrow-based flower of lovely Clarkia has distinctly clawed rose to purple petals. Large godetia has a broader flower with large, rounded petals. They range in color from pinkish to purple-red, often having darker center spots. The flowers mature into leathery quadrangular capsules, releasing small brown seeds by late summer.

The numerous species of *Clarkia* were named after Captain William Clark of the Lewis and Clark expedition.

The seeds are very nutritious and were used by California Indians to make pinole. (See blue dicks.)

Crimson Columbine

Aquilegia formosa var. *truncata*
Blooms: April-June

This beautiful spring wildflower can be found on many moist wooded slopes in the coastal mountains. The nodding flowers often hang over trails and road banks, delighting many a passer-by.

Growing from a woody base, this perennial plant has variously lobed, toothed, basal leaves. Openly branching stems often reach 3 to 5 feet in height. The showy flowers hang singly from the stem, at the outermost tips of the branches. Extending between the spurred red petals are 5 bright orange-red sepals. Long yellow stamens hang down from the center.

Columbine is believed to get its name, *Aquilegia,* from the Latin word for eagle, because the spreading spurs resemble those of an eagle's claws.

Lovely Clarkia

Large Godetia

Crimson Columbine

Wild Ginger

Asarum caudatum
Blooms: March-July

Wild ginger grows in moist shady areas and can be found along many mountain creeks in the northern Coast Ranges.

Its distinctive heart-shaped leaves form a dense carpet, 4 to 6 inches high, on the forest floor. Hiding below these leaves is a small cup-shaped maroon flower formed by long calyx lobes.

Because of the aromatic stems and roots, ginger is widely used in cooking. Early settlers dried and grated the roots for a spice. Candy was made by boiling the roots in sugar. As a medicinal herb, it was considered a remedy for flatulency and whooping cough.

Red Clintonia

Lily Family
Liliaceae Family

Clintonia andrewsiana
Blooms: April-June

Red Clintonia is found near streams and in other moist areas of the redwood and mixed evergreen forests.

Most of the year Clintonia can be identified by its large glossy green basal leaves, which contrast sharply with the darker forest plants. In late spring, a large cluster of deep pink, trumpet-shaped flowers top a long naked stem, which often reaches 2 feet in height. These flowers ripen into dark blue berries from which the plant gets such common names as bead lily and blueing balls.

Wild Ginger

Red Clintonia

Red Clintonia

California Bee-Plant

Scrophularia californica
Blooms: February-July

The California bee plant is common in open places. Because of its weedy nature, it often inhabits disturbed soils such as road banks.

This plant often grows to heights of 3 to 5 feet, easily towering over the other vegetation. The toothed spear-shaped leaves grow oppositely along a square stem. Small, often inconspicuous flowers appear in branched clusters in early spring. The unique flowers have fused petals, forming a small cup with the two upper lips extending outward. The reddish color of the petals and the presence of nectar at the base of each flower attract bees.

Also known by the common name figwort, the plants have the genus name *Scrophularia* because the fleshy underground stems of some species were used to cure the disease scrophula.

Spotted Coral Root

Corallorhiza maculata

Striped Coral Root

Corallorhiza striata
Blooms: April-July

Spotted coral root grows in extremely shady areas, while striped coral root can be found in the more open oak-madrone forests and on dry, brushy slopes. Both species are inconspicuous and seldom seen.

The coral roots are saprophites which, unlike most plants, have no green parts for producing energy from sunlight, but instead receive nutrients from decaying material. Upon casual observation, both plants appear to be nothing more than short, slender, reddish-brown stalks, but closer scrutiny shows the small flowers which are the distinguishing feature between the two species. The petals of spotted coral root are covered with reddish-brown blotches, while striped coral root flower petals have distinct veins of the same color. When the root is exposed it resembles a marine coral, hence the common names.

The Indians believed that these plants had a supernatural origin because of their lack of green parts, so they dried them to make a strengthening tea.

California Bee Plant

Spotted Coral Root

Striped Coral Root

Flowering Currant

Gooseberry Family
Grossulariaceae Family

Ribes glutinosum
Blooms: March-April

Flowering or winter currant is usually found in shaded woods and along streams. It is quite abundant on the trail to Castle Rock at Castle Rock State Park.

This shrub has alternate leaves and, unlike its relative the gooseberry, it has no spines on the stems. The pink flowers hang in clusters from stalks and mature to black berries in summer.

The name currant comes from the Corinth region in England, where plants similar to our currants grow.

Like many other berries, currants are edible either raw or cooked into jams. Many Indians dried these berries, mixed them with animal fat, and stored them for winter use.

California Ground Cone

Broomrape Family
Orobanchaceae Family

Boschniakia strobilacea
Blooms: May-July

Ground cones are parasitic plants which get their nutrients from other plants' roots. This herb associates most often with the roots of madrones and manzanitas, inhabiting dry wooded slopes and chaparral.

Often inconspicuous, the 6 to 10 inch high ground cones are a dark reddish brown and blend with the surrounding duff. The leaves are scale-like, resembling the bracts of a pine cone, hence its common name. Small 2-lipped tubular flowers project between these scales.

Flowering Currant

Flowering Currant
California Ground Cone

California Fuschia

Evening Primrose Family
Onagraceae Family

Zauschneria californica
Blooms: July-November

The California fuschia usually grows in poor, rocky soil in chaparral and other dry areas.

When not flowering, this perennial fuschia is a nondescript gray-green plant which grows in clumps. Its small narrow leaves grow directly off erect stalks, having no leaf stems. Covered with fine white hairs which can vary dramatically in number and size, these leaves are well protected against excessive water loss. The California fuschia is one of the few spectacular blooming plants of late summer and fall. Its trumpet-shaped flowers cover the tops of the erect stems with bright scarlet.

Like our domestic ornamental fuschias, the California fuschia produces nectar which is a major source of energy for hummingbirds. It is especially important since it is one of the few food sources available when they start their southern migration.

California Hedge Nettle

Mint Family
Labiatae Family

Stachys bullata
Blooms: April-September

This native is found in most wooded habitats throughout these coastal mountains. It often forms dense growths or hedges, completely covering moist ravines and slopes.

The slender simple stem of the California hedge nettle has opposite leaves along its length. Covering both stems and leaves are small soft hairs, which, unlike true nettle, don't sting. In spring, flowers are borne on whorls at the top of the stalks. These purplish-red blooms are 2-lipped, like most mints.

The leaves, either soaked or steeped in water, can be used in the treatment of wounds and sores.

California Fuschia

California Hedge Nettle

California Fuschia

Indian Warrior

Figwort Family
Scrophulariaceae Family

Pedicularis densiflora
Blooms: January-July

Found more commonly on the warmer eastern slopes of the mountains, Indian warrior is only occasionally seen in dry oak woodland or chaparral on the western side.

The deep red flowers which call attention to this plant grow in a dense spike atop a 6 to 20 inch tall stem. Several of these flower spikes grow from the base of each plant. The fern-like, finely divided leaves are also mostly basal, although some smaller ones do grow on the erect stem.

According to legend each of these beautiful plants grows for a fallen Indian warrior. The legend behind the genus name isn't quite so romantic. An old superstition that sheep became infested with lice when they ate this plant resulted in the name *Pedicularis,* meaning louse.

Red Larkspur

Buttercup Family
Ranunculaceae Family

Delphinium nudicaule
Blooms: April-June

Red larkspur grows in dry areas in the mixed evergreen forests. Although not commonly seen in all regions, occasional large concentrations of the bright red flowers can be found. The Toll Road Trail in Castle Rock State Park is an especially good place to see these plants.

When not in bloom, red larkspur is an inconspicuous plant with short, lobed leaves. However, in late spring several scarlet red flowers with long spurs appear at the end of a 2 to 3 foot long leafless stalk. A related species, coast larkspur, which is found at Castle Rock State Park, has brilliant blue flowers.

Another name for red larkspur is sleep root, since it was used as a narcotic to dull the senses of gambling opponents by California Indians, who were ardent gamblers.

Indian Warrior

Red Larkspur　　　　　　　　Coast Larkspur

Calypso Orchid

Orchid Family
Orchidaceae Family

Calypso bulbosa
Blooms: March-July

This beautiful plant grows in moist woods and bogs along the northern West Coast. It is extremely rare in the Santa Cruz Mountains, so great care should be taken to preserve the plant when it is found.

The Calypso orchid has a single leaf and a single flower. Growing from a fleshy root stock, the glossy-green basal leaf serves as an early indicator of where the flower will appear. In mid-spring, the pink flower grows atop a slender 4 to 6 inch long stem. The 3 sepals and 2 of the petals extend outward over a third petal. This lower petal is a large, inflated sac-like lip which is mottled pink and white and has a ring of small hairs lining the inner edge.

The orchid gets its common name from the Greek goddess, Calypso.

Chaparral Pea

Pea Family
Fabaceae Family

Pickeringia montana
Blooms: May-August

As its common name implies, chaparral pea is a chaparral shrub, often forming dense thickets. Its colorful flowers brighten up ridgeline trails throughout the mountains.

This plant has small, tough, water conserving leaves and stiff branches. Its sharp spines sometimes stab the unwary hiker. Growing singly along the stems, large showy pink flowers are pea-shaped. As the flower matures a seed pod forms, releasing black, oblong seeds. Chaparral pea easily spreads by underground stems and is well adapted to a fire-burned environment.

Calypso Orchid
Chaparral Pea

Woolly Paint Brush

Figwort Family
Scropulariaceae Family

Castilleja foliolosa
Blooms: March-August

Woolly paintbrush is fairly common on rocky chaparral slopes.

Several erect unbranching stalks with linear, sometimes 3-lobed leaves grow from the woody base of each plant. Covering both stems and leaves, long white hairs form a dense woolly mat and protect against moisture loss. On the upper tips of the stalks are bright scarlet flowers which stand out against the somber chaparral background. Unlike most flowers, it is the sepals and leaf-like bracts below them which are brilliant red, hiding the smaller yellow-green petals.

Since Indian paintbrush is found in rocky chaparral areas which are favorite places for rattlesnakes, they were known by some Indian tribes as "snake's friend." Their bright flowers were thought to be the source of rattlesnake venom. Surprisingly, or perhaps not, they were also used as a love charm.

California Rhododendron

Heath Family
Ericaceae Family

Rhododendron macrophyllum
Blooms: April-July

This showy native inhabits drier slopes of the Santa Cruz Mountains. Found in only a few places, it is a spectacular sight when blooming, with its vibrant color covering the hillside. This species becomes much more common in the damp north coast areas.

The rhododendron is related to the more common western azalea. Often reaching heights of 10 to 12 feet, this evergreen shrub has leathery dark green leaves. Large fragrant clusters of bright pink flowers cover the shrub in late spring, maturing into cylindrical capsules. Brown winged seeds are released in fall.

Many varieties of the rhododendron are used commercially for garden ornamentals.

Woolly
Paint
Brush

California
Rhododendron

Scarlet Pimpernel

Primrose Family
Primulaceae Family

Anagallis arvensis
Blooms: most of the year

Scarlet pimpernel is fairly common in open, dry, disturbed locations such as old pastures and logged areas.

This tiny plant forms mats of growth about 3 inches high. Its angular stem has leaves spaced at regular intervals, usually in whorls of three. Growing on stalks from the base of these leaves are tiny star-shaped orange flowers with purple centers.

Scarlet pimpernel gained fame when an English novel *The Scarlet Pimpernel* was named for it. The hero of the novel was known for his ability to spring from nowhere into a sudden blaze of glory. Like him, the pimpernel seems to come from nowhere to suddenly cover large patches of ground with bright orange flowers. Another romantic aspect of this flower was its enclosure in love letters as a symbol of the writer's passion.

Wood Rose

Rose Family
Rosaceae Family

Rosa gymnocarpa
Blooms: April-September

Wood rose grows in shady areas of redwood and mixed evergreen forests.

A small shrub with slender stems and fine, straight prickles, wood rose grows 2 to 4 feet high. Its leaves, composed of 5 to 7 leaflets each, are arranged alternately along the stem. The dainty pink blossoms are about 1 inch wide. In autumn, these flowers are replaced with red urn-shaped rose hips.

Rose hips, which have 24 times as much vitamin C as oranges, were used by Indians to make a rose colored tea for the relief of colds. Today rose hips are used commercially to make vitamin C tablets.

Some Indian tribes used tea from the leaves to relieve pains and colic. The petals can also be used for tea, as well as eaten raw or in jellies.

Another species of rose, the California rose *(Rosa californica),* is also commonly found in these mountains and has the same uses as wood rose. In comparison with wood rose, the California rose has a fuller, brighter-colored flower, hairy leaf undersides, and curved prickles.

Scarlet Pimpernel

Wood Rose

California Rose

Redwood Sorrel

Oxalis Family
Oxalidaceae Family

Oxalis oregana
Blooms: February-September

Redwood sorrel is extremely abundant in the redwood, mixed ever-green, and redwood streamside forests, often covering the ground in thick carpets.

The clover-like leaves are extremely sun sensitive, folding down like umbrellas whenever it gets too hot. Solitary flowers grow on small stalks and turn from white to deep pink with age.

Both the stems and leaves can be eaten raw in salads or slightly fermented for a tangy dessert. Their sour taste is responsible for the Latin name *Oxalis,* or acid juice. The pioneers used these sour stems in a pie similar to rhubarb pie.

Pacific Starflower

Primrose Family
Primulaceae Family

Trientalis latifolia
Blooms: March-June

The Pacific starflower is commonly found in the redwood, mixed ever-green, and redwood streamside communities. Like redwood sorrel, the starflower often completely covers large areas of ground in these forests.

This plant is easily identified by its small whorl of leaves atop a slender stem, with 1 to 4 tiny pink star-shaped flowers growing from the center. Although somewhat resembling trillium, the starflower has thinner, smaller leaves, with 5 to 7 in a whorl.

Redwood Sorrel
Pacific Starflower

Giant Wake Robin

Lily-of-the-Valley Family
Convallariaceae Family

Trillium chloropetalum
Blooms: February-April

The giant wake robin is usually found on brushy wooded slopes. More common north of San Mateo County, it is seldom seen in the Big Basin State Park area. However, one nice cluster grows next to the Castle Rock State Park parking lot.

Although taller than western wake robin, this plant is similarly characterized by its whorl of 3 large dark green leaves which grow directly from the main stem. The flowers, composed of 3 erect petals, grow directly above these leaves and have no flower stalks. As they mature, the flowers darken to a deep red-purple.

While the deep maroon color of the flowers is common in the central area of these mountains, the more northern flowers are often tinged with green and are responsible for the genus name *Chloropetalum,* meaning green petal. Like western wake robin, the underground stems can cause vomiting if eaten.

Wintergreen

Wintergreen Family
Pyrolaceae Family

Pyrola picta forma *aphylla*
Blooms: June-August

This small herb usually grows on wooded slopes, often associating with Douglas firs and madrones.

Wintergreen, or red pyrola, grows from a slender root, sending up an often leafless stalk 6 to 7 inches in height. The delicate 5-part flowers have red to purple sepals and pink petals, which often have white margins. Giving the flowers a pendant appearance, 10 stamens grow around the long style.

Giant Wake Robin

Wintergreen

Flowers — Blue to Purple

Blue-eyed Grass

Iris Family
Iridaceae Family

Sisyrinchium bellum
Blooms: February-May

Blue-eyed grass is common in open meadow areas, often found associated with oak forests.

This plant is a classic demonstration of the problems with common names. Blue-eyed grass is not a grass at all, but an iris. Rather than having blue "eyes," the flowers are dark purple with yellow "eyes" in the center. These flowers are perched singly on short stalks off the main stem. Long, slender leaves which clasp the stem are often hidden by surrounding grasses. The albino variety in the photograph is quite uncommon, but striking when growing alongside the blue.

Since pigs sometimes grub at the woody roots, the genus name *Sisyrinchium* means pig snout, while the species name *bellum* means handsome.

Tea made from blue-eyed grass was used as an early remedy for fever reduction.

Blue Dicks

Amaryllis Family
Amaryllidaceae Family

Brodiaea pulchella
Blooms: February-May

Blue dicks are found in open grassy areas, often associated with oaks. They are the most common of the *Brodiaeas* found here.

Conspicuous, tightly-clustered purple flowers grow on a naked stem about a foot tall. Much less noticeable are the long slender leaves, which grow from the base of the plant.

The perennial bulbs were known as Indian onions or potatoes. They were dug out with a digging stick, then eaten raw, boiled, or roasted. The small black seeds were roasted like popcorn in a mix called pinole, which is similar to our present day trail mix.

Blue-eyed Grass

Kathy Lyons

Blue Dicks

Blue Witch

Solanum umbelliferum
Blooms: January-September

Blue witch is found on dry rocky slopes in chaparral or in open areas of oak woodlands.

This woody shrub has hairy leaves which are grayish green. The pinwheel-shaped flowers are deep purple with bright yellow anthers. On the base of the petals surrounding the anthers are pairs of small white dots with green spots in their centers.

Although a close relative of the tomato and potato, this plant is poisonous if eaten. The entire plant is high in solanine, an alkaloid which is also present in the leaves and stems of tomatoes and potatoes. Solanine poisoning can cause such minor symptoms as drowsiness, trembling, weakness, nausea, and abdominal pain, or it can lead to serious problems such as paralysis, unconciousness, or death.

California Harebell

Asyneuma prenanthoides
Blooms: June-September

This perennial grows on dry, wooded slopes in redwood and mixed evergreen forests. It is a common summer wildflower.

The California harebell has simple, toothed, lance-shaped leaves growing alternately along a slender stem. Bright blue tubular flowers hang in scattered clusters off the stem. A long central style extends beyond the blue petals, giving it a bell-like appearance.

The family name, Campanulaceae, comes from the Latin word *campana,* meaning little bell. Many species of this family are used as ornamentals.

Western Hound's Tongue

Cynoglossum grande
Blooms: February-April

Hound's tongue is one of the first flowers of spring and is common in wooded mixed evergreen forests throughout these mountains.

This native has large, simple leaves arising mostly from the base of the plant. Small hairs on the surface give the leaf a rough texture. The shape and texture somewhat resemble a dog's tongue, hence the common name. Clusters of small blueish-purple flowers are borne atop a long central stalk and mature into spiny nutlets. The tiny hooks cling easily to animal fur, aiding in seed dispersal.

California Harebell

Blue Witch

**Western
Hound's Tongue**

California Fetid Adder's Tongue

Scoliopus bigelovii
Blooms: February-March

Fetid adder's tongue grows only in moist redwood valleys, especially along streams.

Since this small plant is one of the earliest to flower in the spring, few hikers see the exquisite blooms. Composed of sepals which are stamped with distinct, dark purple veins and erect, dark purple, horn-like petals, the blooms grow on short stalks between the basal leaves. These large oval leaves are pointed at the tip and have purple blotches scattered over the glossy green surface. Individual plants usually bear only 2 leaves, but occasionally have 3.

Although the sight of the flower is a treat, its smell, probably to attract flies as pollinators, is not so pleasant and is responsible for the name fetid adder's tongue. Another common name, slink pod, refers to the fact that the slender stems droop to the ground as the flower pods mature. The genus name *Scoliopus,* meaning crooked foot, also refers to this drooping stem.

Lupine

Lupinus species
Blooms: depends on species

Several species of lupine are found in this area. Although probably most common in open meadows, these plants can be found in almost every habitat from sandy beaches to shady forests. The various species range from being quite common to extremely rare.

Although their growth forms vary from small annual or perennial herbs to large shrubs, lupines have several distinguishable features in common. The leaves, which are always alternate and compound palmate, are the most easily identifiable characteristic of these plants. Also, all lupines have flowers arranged in whorls near the top of erect stems. Individual flowers are pea-like with 5 parts. Reflexed back behind the other petals, the large upper petal is called the banner. In front of this petal are 2 smaller petals called wings which surround 2 even smaller, joined petals called the keel. Most of our local lupines are various shades of lavender to blue, although a few are shades of yellow or white.

The name *Lupinus* comes from lupus, meaning wolf, because these plants were once thought to destroy the soil. However, this couldn't be further from the truth since Lupines help the soil both by stabilizing it with their deep roots, and by building up its nitrogen supply with the bacteria in its root nodules.

Although the seeds reportedly were boiled and used to treat urinary disorders, they often contain dangerous alkaloids.

California Fetid Adder's Tongue

Lupine

California Wild Lilac

Ceanothus species
Blooms: March-August

Lilac is common in drier regions of several communities. It can be found in chaparral, mixed evergreen forests, meadows, oak woodlands, and redwood forests.

Several species of lilac grow in this area, including both the white and the blueish-purple varieties. All species are large woody shrubs with fragrant flower clusters composed of tiny individual flowers.

Warty-leaved ceanothus *(Ceanothus papillosus)* is common in chaparral and along forest margins. Its deep purple flowers and small warty leaves make it the most easily identifiable of the lilacs.

Blue blossom ceanothus *(Ceanothus thyrsiflorus)* is common in more moist, shaded regions of the mountains, sometimes forming almost pure forests with shrubs 20 feet high. Its oval-shaped leaves are bright green and have 3 major veins converging at the base.

Early Indians had several uses for these shrubs. Flowers and leaves were made into tea, while the bark was used to make a tonic. Leaves were used as tobacco and roots made a red dye. Several tribes used the stems as foundations for their baskets.

When the blossoms are mixed with water and rubbed vigorously they make a fragrant soap. In some Indian tribes, this soap was used by the bride and groom to wash each other's hair as part of the wedding ceremony.

Warty-leaved Ceanothus

California Wild Lilac

Henderson's Shooting Star

Primrose Family
Primulaceae Family

Dodecatheon hendersonii
Blooms: February-May

Shooting stars grow on open slopes and in woods in these coastal mountains. Especially large concentrations can be found blooming near small intermittent springs and creeks.

This plant is well known for its attractive and colorful flower clusters. Hanging atop slender stems, they have maroon to purple petals which are bent backwards to a expose dark central stamen. Rings of yellow and black encircle the base of the petals. The glossy green oval leaves have long stems and arise in a cluster around the base.

Either boiled or roasted, the roots and leaves are edible.

California Toothwort

Mustard Family
Cruciferae Family

Dentaria californica var. *californica*
Blooms: December-May

Toothwort is a common inhabitant of all shaded areas within the coastal mountains. Although extremely variable, it is generally one of the earliest spring wildflowers.

This slender plant grows from a fleshy underground stem and has two characteristic leaf patterns. Broad oval leaves arise independently from the root base, while slender lance-shaped leaves grow from the erect, unbranched flower stalk. These generally consist of 3 leaflets. White to lavender 4-part flowers grow in clusters from the top of the stem, maturing into long slim seed pods. Another variety of *Dentaria,* milkmaids (var. *integrifolia*), is also found in this area, and the two freely hybridize.

The rootstocks are edible raw and are often added to salads. The name *Dentaria*, meaning tooth, pertains to these odd-shaped, toothed, underground stems.

Henderson's
Shooting Star

California
Toothwort

Vetch

Vicia species
Blooms: depends on species

Many species of vetch are found in these mountains, most of them natives of Europe. American vetch *(Vicia americana* var. *oregona)* is the most common species. Vetch usually grows along trails and roadsides or in other disturbed areas.

The leaves of this trailing vine are composed of alternate linear leaflets and usually have climbing tendrils. Similar to the garden pea, to which they are related, the flowers of most of our species range from pale lilac to deep red-purple, although a few species have at least some white. The flowers are either arranged in rows on a long stem, or grow singly on short stems from the leaf axis.

The genus name *Vicia* means to bind together and refers to the way in which the tendrils wrap around other plants.

Young seeds and shoots can be cooked and eaten like domestic peas.

Yerba Santa

Eriodictyon californicum
Blooms: April-July

Yerba santa is one of the most abundant plants of the dry chaparral regions. However, it is an opportunist and can occasionally be seen growing along shaded streamsides.

A tall shrub, sometimes reaching 5 feet in height, yerba santa has numerous erect stalks growing from a small short trunk. The main stems are often black from a covering of sooty fungus. Leaves are lance-shaped, thick, and sticky. The tubular flowers are soft lavender and grow in clusters from the tops of the stems.

Yerba santa, meaning holy weed in Spanish, was named by missionaries when they were told by Indians of its many medicinal uses. A bitter tea made from the leaves was used to treat everything from tuberculosis to rheumatism, including coughs, sore throats, and asthma. A weaker tea was used as a blood purifier. Fresh leaves in a poultice were bound on sores, and a strong solution brewed from the leaves was used to soothe sore and tired limbs. Some tribes smoked or chewed these leaves like tobacco.

Vetch

Yerba Santa

Flowers — White to Cream

Bedstraw

Madder Family
Rubiaceae Family

Galium species
Blooms: March-April

Bedstraw grows in moist, shady areas of the redwood and mixed evergreen forests.

It is a spreading vine characterized by square stems and small linear leaves, which grow in whorls around the stems. Because of its small, backward hooks this vine is an excellent climber and often grows over other plants. The tiny, whitish-green flowers grow in clusters of 2 to 5 on a short stalk from the leaf whorl axis.

In some countries this sweet-smelling plant is still used for stuffing mattresses, hence the name bedstraw. One species is even credited with having lined Christ's manger in Bethlehem.

Bedstraw has many other uses. Along with rennet, it was once used in the preparation of cheese. The seeds of some species are used as a coffee substitute when roasted and ground. The roots can be used to make a purple dye.

Coffee Berry

Buckthorn Family
Rhamnaceae Family

Rhamnus californica
Blooms: May-July

The coffee berry is a hardy shrub which prefers dry wooded areas or chaparral. It is commonly seen along many mountain trails.

This shrub has alternate leaves 2 to 5 inches long, and like most dry-region plants the leaves are hard and leathery to prevent moisture loss. In fall clusters of greenish flowers ripen into black berries.

This shrub is a close relative of the cascara shrub which is cultivated commercially and used in the preparation of laxatives. Although the coffee berry is not cultivated, it can be used as a substitute for cascara. The process involves collecting bark in spring or fall, drying it for a year, grinding it into a powder, then mixing it with hot water. Fresh bark can also be used if boiled for a number of hours.

The berries are edible either raw or cooked and are quite nutritious.

Bedstraw

Coffee Berry

Western Azalea

Heath Family
Ericaceae Family

Rhododendron occidentale
Blooms: June-September

Although not particularly common in this area, this shrub sometimes forms dense thickets along streams and moist meadows in redwood and mixed evergreen forests. It is especially prevalent along Opal Creek near Big Basin Park Headquarters.

In spring this large deciduous shrub produces bright green leaves. Unlike its relative, the California rhododendron, the leaves are thin and somewhat glandular.

In locations with ample sunlight, large showy clusters of creamy-white or pinkish-white flowers cover the bush. The strong fragrance from these flowers is a treat for hikers along several mountain trails.

All parts of this plant are poisonous.

Common Buck Brush

Buckthorn Family
Rhamnaceae Family

Ceanothus cuneatus var. *dubius*
Blooms: February-August

As its name implies, common buck bush, one of several white varieties of lilac, is often found in these mountains. It is abundant in chaparral, sometimes forming impenetrable thickets.

This large woody shrub has dark-green smooth-margined leaves which are thick and leathery to minimize water loss. The leaves grow on spine-like branchlets which often spear unwary hikers. The small white flowers grow in fragrant clusters.

For uses of this shrub see the California wild lilac in the blue-flowering section.

Elk Clover

Ginseng Family
Araliaceae Family

Aralia californica
Blooms: July-August

Elk clover, or spikenard, is usually found along streamsides or in very moist redwood or mixed evergreen forests.

This spreading shrub can reach up to 10 feet tall or more. Its alternate leaves have stems as much as 1 foot long. The leaves are compound, consisting of 3 separate groups of leaflets with 3 to 5 leaflets in a group. Individual leaflets can sometimes be as large as 5 inches wide by 7 inches long. In early summer, loose clusters of small white flowers bloom on the tips of the branches. Later these mature into purplish-black berries.

Western
Azalea

Common Buck Brush

Elk Clover

California Blackberry

Rubus ursinus
Blooms: March-August

Blackberries are usually found in sunny areas near water in most of the plant communities. They also sometimes form sprawling thickets in open meadows.

This thorny vine has stout, erect stems entwined with thinner trailing shoots. Most of the leaves are compound with 3 pointed leaflets. However, smaller simple leaves may also be found on flowering stems. Although sometimes confused with poison oak by beginning botanists, blackberry leaves and stems have thin prickles, while poison oak does not. The white rose-like flowers produce juicy black berries in late summer.

The most common use of blackberries is as a food, either eaten raw or cooked in pies, jellies, or preserves. Also, young shoots can be sliced and eaten in salads. Blackberry brandy was used by early settlers as an efficient cure for diarrhea. A less familiar use was in the making of a black dye for basketry by the Luiseno Indians (a West Coast tribe).

Chamise

Adenostoma fasciculatum
Blooms: May-June

Chamise is one of the most common shrubs in the dry rocky chaparral communities, especially in recently burned areas. The most dramatic display of chamise is from the face of the Skyline-to-the-sea Trail at Castle Rock State Park. In August the surrounding hillsides have turned a beautiful rusty-orange from the dried chamise flowers.

Well adapted to the dry sunny habitats in which it grows, chamise has small, thick, leathery leaves. The highly branched stems are capable of regeneration by stump sprouting after a fire. In addition, this shrub exhibits an interesting survival mechanism called alleopathy, which is characteristic of many chaparral plants. Growth-inhibiting toxins are produced in the leaves, then washed into surrounding soil during rains to eliminate close competition.

In early summer, tiny white flowers grow profusely in panicles on the upper stems.

Although this tough plant isn't much of a delicacy, young stems can be tenderized by boiling for several hours, then seasoned, and eaten like a vegetable.

California Blackberry
Chamise

California Blackberry

Chinese Houses

Figwort Family
Scrophulariaceae Family

Collinsia heterophylla
Blooms: April-July

Chinese houses inhabit open or shaded slopes throughout the coastal mountains. They are often associated with oak woodlands and grassy knolls.

This annual grows from ½ to 1 foot in height. Slightly toothed, oblong leaves grow opposite on the slender stem. Blooming in late spring, clusters of 2 to 5 flowers grow in whorls. The individual flower parts are fused, forming 2 major lips. The upper lip is usually whitish and the lower lip is a deep lavender. The beautiful shape gives the plant its common name, for they resemble Chinese pagodas.

Poison Hemlock

Parsley Family
Umbelliferae Family

Conium maculatum
Blooms: April-August

Poison hemlock needs a sunny, open area to grow, and therefore is often found in areas which have been disturbed by humans. The plant is especially abundant in the meadow by the Butano State Park entrance.

This tall plant has parsley-like leaves with a smooth, purple-splotched stem. These stems can grow 10 to 12 feet high, terminating in large, white, umbel-shaped flower heads.

This native of Europe is extremely poisonous, producing instant paralysis resulting in death. Since hemlock somewhat resembles the edible cow parsnip and sweet fennel, novice gatherers should beware. Legend has it that poison hemlock was used to poison Socrates and to this day its purple-blotched stem is branded by his blood.

Inside-Out Flower

Barberry Family
Berberidaceae Family

Vancouveria planipetala
Blooms: April-September

The inside-out flower inhabits moist areas, often associating with year-round streams and creeks. Many are found growing within the redwood community along Berry Creek Falls Trail in Big Basin.

These small delicate white flowers are rather inconspicuous. Growing from thin branching stems, they have reflexed sepals and petals that expose the central stamens, giving the blooms the appearance of being inside-out. The finely-toothed leaves grow off thin black stems, resembling those of maidenhair fern.

Inside-out Flower

Poison Hemlock

Chinese Houses

Globe Lily

Calochortus albus
Blooms: April-May

Globe lilies grow in shaded dry areas under oak or mixed evergreen forests. Since they are somewhat uncommon and inconspicuous except when blooming, these small plants are seldom seen.

Globe lilies are bulb plants distinguished by a long, single, linear leaf growing from the base, with smaller leaves growing along the stem. The slender stems have nodding white flowers which branch off on short stalks. They are also known as fairy lanterns because of their resemblance to lantern globes.

The perennial bulbs are nutritious and were eaten by California Indians. Although edible raw, they were most often boiled, roasted or steamed in fire pits. Dried, they could be ground into flour for later use. Because of the globe lilies' limited distribution and the numerous other food sources available, these beautiful flowers should be left for all others to enjoy.

Hooker's Fairy Bells

Disporum hookeri
Blooms: March-May

Hooker's fairy bells have a wide range of habitats. They can be found in shady areas of redwood and mixed evergreen forests and also in oak woodlands.

This low-spreading plant is sometimes confused with Solomon's seal. However, it can be distinguished by its branching form. Small greenish-white flowers hang in pairs from the terminal leaves like hidden bells. In late summer, the flowers ripen to bright scarlet berries.

The two seeds in each cavity of its ovary give Hooker's fairy bells their genus name *Disporum,* while their species name is in honor of W.J. Hooker, a famous English botanist.

Globe Lily
Hooker's Fairy Bells

Hooker's Fairy Bells

Western Coltsfoot

Sunflower Family
Groundsel Tribe
Compositae Family

Petasites frigidus var. *palmatus*
Blooms: March-May

Coltsfoot is common in redwood forests along streamsides. It seems to be especially abundant along Little Butano Creek in Butano State Park and along upper Waddell Creek in Big Basin Redwoods State Park.

Deeply lobed, palmate leaves grow at the end of a 6-inch long stem which rises directly from the perennial rootstock. The leaf undersides are covered with soft white hairs. Blossoming at the end of a long stem with leaf-like bracts, the white flowers appear somewhat like tightly-clustered dandelion seed heads.

Indians living away from the ocean had an interesting use for the plant. They would place the wilted leaves on a redwood burl over hot coals. In the slow heat of the fire the leaves burned down to ashes of almost pure salt.

Huckleberry

Huckleberry Family
Vacciniaceae Family

Vaccinium ovatum
Blooms: February-June

Although most often found in redwood and mixed evergreen forests, huckleberry is extremely adaptable and can also be seen in chaparral. It grows profusely near headquarters in Portola and Big Basin State Parks, and along the entire Coast Range.

This woody evergreen shrub forms large thickets which cover the forest floor. The alternate dark green leaves are thick and leathery enough to survive chaparral conditions. In spring small white bell-shaped flowers hang below the branches, then ripen to deep blue berries in autumn. With the extra sunlight received, the chaparral area plants tend to have much sweeter berries.

Except for 10 small, hard seeds, the fruit is much like blueberries and has the same uses. The berries are excellent raw, or cooked in pies, preserves, and jellies. In some places they are grown commercially. As the story goes, Mark Twain so relished huckleberry preserves that he named one of his most famous characters, Huckleberry Finn, after the plant.

Western Coltsfoot

Huckleberry

Miner's Lettuce

Purselane Family
Portulacaceae Family

Montia perfoliata
Blooms: February-May

Miner's lettuce is fairly common in moist wooded areas.

This plant is easily identifiable by its united saucer-like leaves which grow on 3 to 8 inch long stems. Tiny white flowers bloom on stalks from the leaf centers.

As the name implies, miner's lettuce can be eaten raw in salads or boiled like spinach. A common practice of California Indians was to place the plant near red ant hills. As the ants crawled over the leaves, they left behind a vinegary flavor like a salad dressing.

The Indians also made a tea from the leaves, which was used as a laxative.

Mountain Iris

Iris Family
Iridaceae Family

Iris douglasiana
Blooms: April-June

Mountain iris commonly grows in mixed evergreen forest, grassland, and open woodland. It is especially prevalent in Big Basin along Berry Creek and Sunset Trails as well as in the Slippery Rock area.

The showy flowers range from blue to cream-white and are situated atop tall, fibrous stalks, sometimes with side branches. As is typical with all irises, the leaves clasp to the stem, which can be from 12 to 24 inches in height.

The fibers from the side ribs of the leaves were often twisted together by Indians to make a surprisingly strong string or rope. For small-game hunting, a *bola* was made by hanging small bones from the ends of the string. This was then swung toward the animal, entangling it and bringing it down. The tan-colored string was also woven together to form fishing nets and game snares. The northern Indians used young leaves as a wrap for their babies.

It should also be noted that all parts of the Iris are poisonous.

Miner's Lettuce

Mountain Iris

Mountain Iris

Manzanita

Arctostaphylos species
Blooms: various species bloom from November-May

Manzanita is one of the most common shrubs in chaparral. It grows on almost every dry ridgeline in the mountains.

These shrubs seem to be undergoing rapid evolution which results in many species, some of which are very similar and some very different. This makes it difficult to distinguish between species. However, all are characterized by reddish bark, with an outer skin which periodically peels off. Thick, leathery leaves are arranged alternately on the woody stems. Small clusters of bell-shaped flowers hang from the terminal tips of the branches.

Manzanita means little apple in Spanish and was so named because of its berries. Like several other wild berries, these fruits are edible and can be eaten raw or cooked in preserves, pies, and stews. When scalded, crushed, and strained they make a spicy cider, and can also be made into wine.

One species of manzanita has leaves and bark which were used as tobacco by West Coast Indians. Its leaves were also used for treatment of urinary tract disorders and are still used today as an ingredient in astringents. Because of the high tannic acid content of the leaves, they were once used in the tanning industry and are still so used in Russia.

Stinging Nettle

Urtica holosericea
Blooms: May-October

Nettles grow along streams and in moist redwood forests.

These plants have large spear-shaped opposite leaves which are coarsely toothed. They grow to almost 6 feet in height and are covered with small poison-filled hairs which inflict extremely painful stings. White flower clusters hang from the junction of leaves and stems.

Despite the sharp poison hairs, nettle leaves and stems are edible when steamed or boiled and make a good spinach substitute. A mixture of salt and a strong solution of nettle was used to make rennet.

Some European species were used to make a cloth which was stronger than cotton linen. Indians also used the stem fibers in their basket weaving and obtained a yellow dye from the roots.

Manzanita

Manzanita

Stinging Nettle

Western Morning Glory

Convolvulus occidentalis
Blooms: April-July

Western morning glory, a native, grows in brushy areas or open woods. It is especially common in chaparral and disturbed areas.

This woody climbing vine is often found entangled in other shrubs. Its triangular leaves are alternate. Creating quite a splash of color on the brown hillsides, the large funnel-shaped flowers turn from white to purple with age.

The genus name *Convolvulus* means to entwine and refers to the twisted, twining stems.

The seeds were once used as a narcotic.

Black Sage

Mint Family
Labiatae Family

Salvia mellifera
Blooms: March-August

Black sage is a common inhabitant of the chaparral. It is especially abundant along the dry, south-facing slopes of Castle Rock and Big Basin State Parks.

This shrub has oppositely arranged oblong leaves which have slightly toothed margins. The aromatic leaves, characteristic of the mint family, are a distinguishing feature. Whitish to pale blue tubular flowers grow in clusters along a tall stem, often reaching high above surrounding plants.

The seeds of black sage were used to flavor food by early Californians, who added them to cooking meats and poultry. A tea can be made by soaking these seeds in water.

Pitcher Sage

Mint Family
Labiatae Family

Lepechinia calycina
Blooms: April-July

This perennial sage commonly grows in chaparral communities of the Santa Cruz Mountains and also occasionally inhabits the edges of dry mixed evergreen forests. It is especially prevalent along China Grade in Big Basin State Park and along the Skyline-to-the-Sea Trail in Castle Rock State Park.

Pitcher sage grows as a medium-sized shrub. The aromatic leaves are slightly toothed and covered with small hairs. Characteristic of most of the mint family, the stems are square. Single, white, tubular flowers appear in mid-spring, attracting numerous bees to their nectar.

Western Morning Glory

Black Sage
Pitcher Sage

Salal

Gaultheria shallon
Blooms: April-July

Salal is a fairly common plant of the redwood and mixed evergreen forest floors. It can often be seen hanging over trail ledges, and stream and road banks.

This plant grows as a low-spreading shrub. Ranging in length from 2 to 4 inches, the thick, dark-green leaves are oblong with pointed tips. The pinkish bell-shaped flowers appear in late spring and hang in rows off a central axis. With the onset of summer, berries replace the flower groups and turn black when ripe.

The berries are edible either raw or cooked into jam and pies.

Soap Plant

Chlorogalum pomeridianum
Blooms: May-June

Soap plant is found on dry slopes, often intermixed with plants of the chaparral. It is common throughout the coastal mountains.

This perennial lily grows from an underground bulb and produces a cluster of basal leaves each fall. These conspicuous leaves are long and narrow with characteristic wavy margins. In late spring, clusters of small white flowers are borne atop a tall branching stem. These delicate flowers are rarely seen by hikers, since they open only in the early evening or on cloudy days.

There are numerous uses for the soap plant. The leaves, when picked young, produce a green dye that California Indians used in tattooing and are edible either raw or cooked. Uncooked bulbs, containing saponin, a lather-producing substance, can be crushed and used for shampoo and soap. Indians baked the starchy bulbs and ate them like potatoes. When cooked slowly, they lost their soapiness and were quite nutritious. As the bulbs were roasted, a thick substance was exuded which was collected and used as glue to attach feathers to hunting arrows.

Much like buckeye nuts, the bulbs of the soaproot were used to catch fish. Crushed bulbs thrown into water stupified fish so that they could be easily gathered. Although this procedure numbed the nervous system of the fish, it apparently had no effect on their edibility. It should be noted that because this type of fishing deteriorates the quality of lakes and streams, and kills all aquatic life, it is illegal in California.

Salal

Soap Plant
Soap Plant

Rein Orchid

Orchid Family
Orchidaceae Family

Habenaria unalascensis
Blooms: April-September

Rein orchids grow on fairly dry soils, often within the mixed evergreen and oak woodlands.

These small plants grow as simple, erect stalks up to 12 inches high. Linear leaves, usually 2 to 4 in number, arise from the stem base. Covering the top of the spike in tightly packed clusters are greenish-white spurred flowers.

Either raw or cooked, the tuberous roots are edible. However, since these orchids are not very widespread, they should not be disturbed.

Phantom Orchid

Orchid Family
Orchidaceae Family

Cephalanthera austinae
Blooms: May

This orchid inhabits dry woods along the northern coastal mountains but is extremely rare. It grows in only a few locations in the Santa Cruz Mountains.

The phantom orchid, a saprophyte, obtains its nutrients from dead organic matter in the soil. Growing as a nearly leafless stalk, this white plant reaches 10 to 15 inches in height. The few leaves which are present on the lower part of the stem are reduced to sheaths. Clusters of 2-lipped flowers, flecked with yellow centers, attach closely to the stem.

Because of this plant's ghostly appearance on the forest floor, it is aptly named the phantom orchid.

Western Wake Robin

Lily-of-the-Valley Family
Convallariaceae Family

Trillium ovatum
Blooms: March-May

The wake robin is common in shady redwood forests. It grows especially well in valleys along the many mountain streams.

This small plant is characterized by a whorl of 3 large, dark-green leaves atop a 5 to 8 inch stem. On a short, slender stalk above the leaves is a small, 3-petaled flower, which changes from white to purple as it ages. The name *Trillium* refers to the fact that the leaves and flower parts are in threes.

The thick, fleshy, underground stems cause violent vomiting when eaten.

Phantom Orchid

Rein Orchid

Western Wake Robin

Hairy Star Tulip

Lily Family
Liliaceae Family

Calochortus tolmiei
Blooms: April-June

This member of the lily family is common in open sunny locations, often inhabiting roadside embankments or lightly wooded hillsides.

The hairy star tulip has long, linear leaves and, like other lilies, grows from an underground bulb. Growing on stems 4 to 8 inches long, the beautiful whitish flowers have petals tinged with lavender in the center and covered with soft, bristly hairs. These characteristic hairs also give it the common name of pussy ears. Three-lobed seed capsules replace the flowers when mature.

The scientific name, *Calochortus,* comes from the Greek words *kalos,* meaning beautiful, and *chortos,* meaning grass and refers to the beauty of the flowers and the grass-like appearance of the leaves.

Sugar-scoop

Saxifrage Family
Saxifragaceae Family

Tiarella unifoliata
Blooms: May-July

These small plants grow in shaded areas, often along streams and moist slopes.

Sugar-scoops have deeply lobed, long stemmed, basal leaves with toothed margins. The leaves are covered with small hairs, giving them a soft texture. Small white flowers grow in narrow panicles along a central stem, later maturing into capsules. The appearance of these capsules resembles the shape of a sugar scoop, hence the common name.

Numerous other members of the Saxifrage family have similar leaf and flower characteristics. Alum root, fringe cups, brookfoam, woodland star and California saxifrage are difficult to distinguish without a detailed key, but are also quite common in the coastal mountains.

Hairy
Star Tulip

Sugar-scoop

Two-eyed Violet

Viola ocellata
Blooms: March-June

The two-eyed violet is common on shaded slopes in mixed evergreen forests throughout the coastal mountains.

Growing from a thick fleshy underground root stock, this plant reaches 5 to 10 inches in height. It has bright green heart-shaped leaves which grow either basally or along short branching stems. The delicate flowers have 5 petals, the lower 3 white and the upper 2 white on the inside and purple on the outside. Purple veins line the lower central petal, and the other two lower petals each have single purple spots. These spots, or eyes, give this plant its common name.

Violets have nectar at the base of each flower. The purple veins and spots on the petals serve to attract bee pollinators to the nectar supply. Like its relative the redwood violet, the leaves of these plants are high in vitamins A and C.

Poison Oak

Rhus diversiloba
Blooms: March-May

This well known plant grows in a great variety of habitats throughout the coastal mountains. They are equally at home from dry chaparral to moist, shady redwood forests.

Poison oak has many diverse growth forms, ranging from bushy shrubs to long vines. These vines can have extremely stout stems several inches in diameter and can grow up the sides of trees 40 feet tall or more. All variations have 3-lobed leaves, small whitish flowers, and white berries in summer. They all have skin-irritating oils in the leaves and stems.

In spite of its poison, this plant has many cultural uses. Early Indians, being largely unaffected by the poison, used the stems for thread, warp, and foundation in their baskets, and the juice to dye weaving material black. They also were known to draw patterns on their faces with poison oak juice, then tattoo them with a sooty California nutmeg needle, thereby getting an unfading blueish-green tattoo. Medicinally the juice from the stems, leaves, and roots was used as a cure for warts and ringworm, and as an antidote for rattlesnake venom.

Two Eyed Violet

Poison Oak
Poison Oak

Thimbleberry

Rose Family
Rosaceae Family

Rubus parviflorus var. *velutinus*
Blooms: March-August

The thimbleberry is extremely common in moist redwood and mixed evergreen forests.

Thimbleberry shrubs can reach 3 to 4 feet tall, forming dense thickets. Its large palmate leaves are covered with soft woolly hairs. Simple rose-like flowers appear in spring, later ripening to hollow berries. These thimble-shaped berries give the plant its name.

As with many other berries, these fruits are edible both raw or cooked into jams and pies. Instead of using rouge, pioneer women reddened their cheeks by rubbing them with soft, hairy thimbleberry leaves.

Toyon

Apple Family
Malaceae Family

Photinia arbutifolia
Blooms: June-July

The toyon or Christmas berry shrub is common in chaparral and as an understory in open wooded forests.

This native evergreen shrub is sometimes mistaken for a young tan oak tree. Like the tan oak, the leaves are glossy green, brittle, and toothed. However, a closer look shows that toyon leaves have veins which diverge before reaching the margin, and are more finely-toothed than tan oak leaves. In early summer clusters of drooping white flowers appear, then in late November and early December they ripen into large clusters of bright red berries.

Although today the berries are used mainly for decorations at Christmas, they were once used by both Indians and Spanish Californians as food. The Spanish ate them after boiling in water, then steaming them in a hot cloth for two hours. Another cooking technique was to sprinkle them with sugar and roast them, covered with cloth, in a slow-cooking oven.

Like the Spanish, the Indians rarely ate the berries raw due to their bitter taste when fresh. Instead, they either hung branches over hot coals, or tossed individual berries in a cooking basket along with coals or hot pebbles.

The Indians also made a tea from the bark and leaves which was used in the treatment of assorted aches and pains.

Thimbleberry

Thimbleberry
Toyon

Wood Strawberry

Fragaria californica
Blooms: January-June

Wild strawberries are often found in shaded woods, or near streams.

These small plants can propagate by growing runners which take root and grow more plants. Their leaves, composed of 3-toothed leaflets, arise directly from the base. White rose-like flowers grow singly on separate stems. In early summer, these delicate blooms ripen into small scarlet berries.

The berries are juicy and delicious both raw or cooked into preserves and pies. They are high in vitamin C, thiamin, niacin, and riboflavin. Some Indians also used the green leaves in tea for the treatment of dysentery.

Slim Solomon's Seal

Smilacina stellata var. *sessilifolia*
Blooms: February-March

This herb is common in shady mixed evergreen and redwood forests.

Although it has the same growth form as fat Solomon's seal, slim Solomon's seal has longer, narrower leaves which don't clasp the stem. It also has fewer flowers which grow in clusters off the tip of the stem. These blossoms mature into green berries striped with red.

The unusual common name was given to this plant because it resembles the East Coast Solomon's seal whose flowers mimic the mystic double-triangle symbol called Solomon's seal.

The genus name *Smilacina* means scraper and refers to the hairy stems of some species.

Wood Strawberry

Slim Solomon's Seal
Slim Solomon's Seal

Fat Solomon's Seal

Lily-of-the-Valley Family
Convallariaceae Family

Smilacina racemosa var. *amplexicaulis*
Blooms: March-May

Fat Solomon's seal is common in shady mixed evergreen and redwood forests.

The large oval leaves of this herb are pointed at the tip and clasp around the distinct, unbranched stem. Growing on tiny stalks off the main stem, numerous white flowers cover the tips of the stems for 2 to 4 inches. In summer, these flowers ripen into bright scarlet berries.

These berries are edible and tasty, but somewhat cathartic. After soaking in lye to remove the bitterness, then parboiling to remove the lye, the starchy rootstocks can be eaten; young shoots can also be boiled and eaten.

Star Lily

Bunch Flower Family
Melanthaceae Family

Zygadenus fremontii
Blooms: February-September

Usually found on grassy or brushy slopes, the star lily is most conspicuous after a fire. It also often grows on dry ridges under madrone and tan oak forests.

Star lily is a bulbous plant with narrow linear leaves growing from the base. Its star-shaped white flowers grow in a cluster on top of a tall stalk, which often reaches to 1 or 2 feet in height.

This plant is related to the death camas, which has an extremely poisonous bulb.

It receives its genus name *Zigadenus,* meaning join-gland, from the small gland at the base of each petal. Its species name is in honor of John C. Fremont, a famous pioneer explorer.

Fat Solomon's Seal
Fat Solomon's Seal

Star Lily

Common Yarrow

Sunflower Family
Mayweed Tribe
Compositae Family

Achillea millefolium
Blooms: April-July

As its name indicates, common yarrow is abundant in all dry areas.

A dense cluster of tiny white flowers grows on the top of a slender 1½ to 3 foot tall stalk. Soft, feather-like basal leaves grow to be about 8 inches long.

Used by ancient people to treat colds, fevers, and other ailments, yarrow has been known for centuries as a remedy. However, care should be taken in its use since it may contain some alkaloid poisons.

Its genus name *Achillea* is for Achilles, who, it was said, used a species of yarrow to treat the wounds of his warriors. The species name *millefolium* means thousand-leaved and refers to the very finely-divided basal leaves.

Yerba de Selva

Hydrangea Family
Hydrangeaceae Family

Whipplea modesta
Blooms: March-June

Yerba de selva is common in shady redwood and mixed evergreen forests. However, it is somewhat inconspicuous except when blooming.

This dainty plant has such a tiny stem that it can usually be found drooping almost to the ground. At the end of the stem is a cluster of tiny white flowers. Leaves are about an inch and a half long and very slender.

Its Spanish name means "weed of the forest," while its genus name is in honor of Lieutenant Whipple, commander of an 1850s Pacific Railroad expedition.

Common
Yarrow

Yerba de Selva

Flowers — Yellow to Orange

Buttercup

Buttercup Family
Ranunculaceae Family

Ranunculus californicus
Blooms: February-May

Buttercups are found on woody, grassy slopes which are moist in spring. In fact, the Latin name *Ranunculus* means little frog, because both are found in this habitat.

The compound leaves are basal, lobed, and somewhat variable. The glossy bright lemon-yellow flowers grow on long stems and are shaped like little saucers.

Indians boiled the roots like potatoes. They also tossed seeds in a basket on a windy day to clean them, then placed them in a basket with slow-burning coals, tossing them again as they roasted. Roasting removed the poisonous toxin, protoanemonim, and gave the seeds a popcorn-like flavor. After this preparation the seeds were eaten whole or ground into flour.

Western settlers pickled the young flowers. Also, a yellow dye was made by the Indians by crushing and washing the flowers.

Sticky Monkey Flower

Figwort Family
Scrophulariaceae Family

Diplacus aurantiacus
Blooms: March-July

Sticky monkey flower is a hardy plant found in most dry chaparral regions in these mountains.

It is composed of woody, branched stalks with opposite, narrow, dark green leaves. These thick sticky leaves give the plant its name. In spring the entire stalk is covered with bright orange tubular flowers. These funnel shaped flowers have two lips, with the upper one slightly longer than the lower.

Although bitter, young leaves and stems can be eaten in salads. Indians crushed the raw leaves and stems and applied them to wounds. In early spring the flowers contain a drop of sweet nectar at the base.

Buttercup

Sticky Monkey Flower

California Flannel Bush

Cacao Family
Sterculiaceae Family

Fremontodendron californicum
Blooms: May-June

This shrub grows on dry slopes, often on the edges of seasonal creeks.

The California flannel bush gets its common name from the fuzzy texture of its leaves. Covered with small tufts of hairs on the upper and lower surfaces, the 3-lobed leaves have a dull-green appearance. Large showy yellow flowers bloom in spring, bringing a sudden surge of color to the hillsides. As the flower matures, bristly brown seed capsules form, often remaining on the branches for many months.

The bark of the flannel bush was used by early California settlers for its soothing qualities. Brewed into a tea, the mucilaginous inner bark relieved sore throats and raw membranes. This often gave it another name, slippery elm.

Bush Poppy

Poppy Family
Papaveraceae Family

Dendromecon rigida
Blooms: April-July

Bush poppy is common in sandy or rocky soils, often in recently burned areas. It is usually associated with chaparral or closed-cone pine forests.

The bright yellow, cup-shaped flowers of this shrub are a sharp contrast with the grayish-green growth of the chaparral. Three to 4 foot tall stems are woody, with dull green, willow-like leaves.

The poppy flowers were used as a narcotic.

Redwood Violet

Violet Family
Violaceae Family

Viola sempervirens
Blooms: February-June

Found in moist areas of the redwood forests, redwood violets can be seen throughout these mountains. They are especially abundant in valley floors along creeks.

The violet is a short-stemmed plant with small, heart-shaped leaves. Its tiny flowers are lemon-yellow with purple veins lining the lower 3 petals.

The species name for redwood violet, *sempervirens,* means evergreen.

Violets are related to pansies and are best known as ornamentals. They have also been used to make candied violets, violet-flavored vinegar, and violet leaf tea. However, violets are not very common in these mountains, so it would be a shame to pick them for this purpose.

California Flannel Bush
Bush Poppy

Redwood Violet

Skunk Cabbage

Lysichiton americanum
Blooms: March-June

This herbaceous plant inhabits wet, boggy areas in the coastal mountains. Often found near springs and year-round creeks, large patches grow within the redwood community in Butano and Fall Creek State Parks.

Skunk cabbage is a perennial plant arising from a fleshy, horizontal root. The large, simple, basal leaves are oblong, and often reach 1 to 3 feet in length. Like its relative, the ornamental calla lily, flowers are situated along a fleshy central stem, called a spadix, and surrounded by a large, single leaf, called the spathe. Both the spadix and spathe of skunk cabbage are bright yellow, contrasting beautifully with the deep green leaves. The odorous spathe gives this plant its common name.

Due to the presence of calcium oxalate, a compound that causes choking and burning of the mouth and throat, it is essential that all portions of skunk cabbage be thoroughly cooked before eating. After boiling with several water changes, the leaves are edible as greens. The starchy roots are also edible when roasted, dried, and ground into a flour. However, since patches of skunk cabbage are extremely rare in these mountains, they should not be collected.

California Poppy

Eschscholzia californica
Blooms: March-October

Well adapted to dry areas, the California poppy is common on the chaparral slopes and along roadsides.

Each plant produces several satiny, bright orange, cup-shaped flowers, each on a separate stalk. After blooming, these flowers mature into long seed pods containing numerous seeds. The basal leaves are dull green and are so finely divided that they appear feathery.

Because of its abundance and bright appearance, the poppy is well known as the state flower of California.

It is also known for its narcotic properties which it shares with other members of this family. The leaves were crushed and packed around aching teeth to kill pain. Today the drug is still used in some places as a headache cure.

Skunk Cabbage

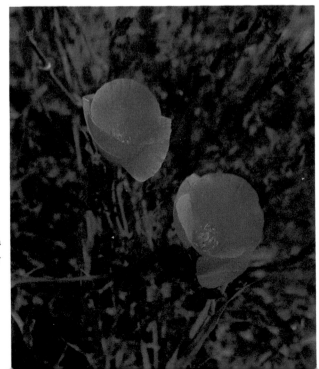

California
Poppy

Checker Lily

Fritillaria lanceolata
Blooms: March-May

Although it sometimes grows on dry open slopes, the checker lily is usually found in the shade of redwood and mixed evergreen forests.

When not blooming, all that can be seen of the checker lily is a large oval basal leaf. However, in early spring a 1 to 2 foot long stem grows from the small subterranean bulbs. On the upper portion of this stem are several whorls of 3 to 5 lance-shaped leaves. Unless seen together, it is hard to believe these leaves grow from the same bulb as the basal leaf. Near the tip of the stem nod greenish-yellow flowers with purple spots. Because of these bell-shaped flowers, another name for this plant is mission bells.

Since the bulbs of most species in this genus are edible either raw, boiled, or dried, the checker lily is probably no exception. Care should be taken, however, since some individuals may not be able to handle large quantities. Because of this, and the fact that these flowers are so beautiful, we recommend they not be eaten.

Tiger Lily

Lilium pardalinum
Blooms: June-September

The tiger lily grows in moist shady areas of redwood and mixed evergreen forests, usually along streams. Once common in these mountains, it was uprooted and taken home by so many people that it is now rather uncommon.

The beautiful orange flowers are marked with purple spots and nod at the end of a stout stem. This stem is 2 to 3 feet tall and has several whorls of long, narrow leaves.

Legend has it that the tiger lily was created by a Korean hermit who removed an arrow from a tiger. They became friends, and when the tiger died, the hermit transformed his body into a tiger lily to preserve their friendship. Later, when the hermit drowned, the tiger lily spread down the streams looking for his lost friend.

Checker Lily

Tiger Lily

Ferns and Fern Allies

Bracken Fern
Fern Family
Polypodiaceae Family

Pteridium aquilinum var. *pubescens*

This is probably the most common fern in the Santa Cruz Mountains. It can be found anywhere from dry, open slopes to moist, sheltered valleys.

In spring, the young fronds uncurl and develop into the adult plants which can be distinguished from other ferns by their highly branched form. Usually 1 to 4 feet tall, the main stem branches laterally to smaller stems from which grow highly divided, leaf-like pinnae. Conspicuous spores mature in small encasings on the undersides of the pinnae in late spring and early summer.

Young fronds are edible and can be eaten raw or steamed. They have a mucilaginous quality which makes them ideal for thickening soups. In fact, the Japanese so relished them that their government had to pass laws to prevent the fern's extinction.

Some references claim that older fronds are only poisonous when eaten in large quantities for an extended length of time. However, eating any part of this plant, except young fronds less than a foot high, is not recommended, since the shoots accumulate a vitamin B-destroying enzyme as they mature.

The roots were used to make basket patterns by some Indian tribes. When raw they produce a brown color, and when boiled, a black color.

Large mature fronds were also used by early settlers to thatch cabin roofs.

Coffee Fern
Fern Family
Polypodiaceae Family

Pellaea andromedaefolia

Coffee fern is one of the few ferns which is found in dry, sunny areas. It is usually found in rocky locations in chaparral.

This hardy fern is generally under 10 inches in height. Small stems grow from the creeping rhizome and branch 2 to 4 times. Growing from these stems are tiny, rounded pinnae, which have a slightly reddish tinge.

The scientific name *Pellea* is a derivation of the Greek word *pellos*, meaning dusky, and refers to the appearance of the stems.

Bracken Fern

Coffee Fern

California Polypody

Fern Family
Polypodiaceae Family

Polypodium californicum

The California polypody is fairly sun tolerant but prefers shady locations. It is found in wooded valleys, often growing on rocks or trees.

This fern is unbranched, with the leaf-like pinnae growing directly along the main stem. The rounded tip of the pinnae is one of the distinguishing features of this fern. Also important for identification are the round clusters of unenclosed spores on the underside of the pinnae.

The California polypody derives its name from the Greek words *polys,* meaning many, and *podi,* meaning foot, because of the many knobby branches of the rhizome.

Western Chain Fern

Fern Family
Polypodiaceae Family

Woodwardia fimbriata

The Western chain fern prefers moist, shady locations and is fairly common along many mountain streams.

This large fern consists of fronds which can reach 6 feet in height. The deeply divided pinnae grow in an orderly, opposite pattern, decreasing in size from the base of the frond to the tip. Spores, encased in a small brown flap called an indusium, grow in a chain-like pattern along the lower midrib of the pinnae.

These ferns were used in basket making. Patterns were made by either using the stems naturally or by dying them red with alder bark.

California
Polypody

Western
Chain Fern

Five-finger Fern

Fern Family
Polypodiaceae Family

Adiantum pedatum var. *aleuticum*

The five-finger fern grows in extremely moist areas, and is usually found alongside streams.

Like the Western maidenhair fern to which it is closely related, the five-finger fern has long slender black stems growing from a scaly base. Each of these stems ends in a palmate, or finger-like, pattern of approximately 5 to 7 smaller stems. These stems have frilly, elongated pinnae which grow asymmetrically. Like the maidenhair, the margins are curled under, hiding the spores.

The long stem of the five-finger fern was used in Indian basketry to make a black pattern. In some areas, these baskets had a special ceremonial purpose. They were used to hold the obsidian knives which were displayed in a jumping dance.

Deer Fern

Fern Family
Polypodiaceae Family

Blechnum spicant

The deer fern inhabits the banks of shady streams in redwood and mixed evergreen forests. Although somewhat uncommon in these mountains, large concentrations do grow along Union and Berry Creeks in Big Basin Redwoods State Park.

This medium-sized fern has small, dark-green pinnae which grow along a central stem. The erect fronds grow in two forms, either sterile or fertile. The sterile evergreen fronds, ranging from 7 to 40 inches in height, have short basal stalks with numerous broad pinnae. These pinnae are crowded along the stem and begin almost from the base of the plant. The fertile fronds are taller, with narrow pinnae growing along the upper two-thirds of a long, naked stalk. Spores develop in small clusters, called sori, and are arranged in parallel rows along the midrib of the fertile pinnae.

Five-finger
Fern

Deer
Fern

Goldenback Fern

Fern Family
Polypodiaceae Family

Pityrogramma triangularis

The goldenback fern often inhabits shaded spots in mixed evergreen and oak forests. Occasionally it can also be found on dry brushy slopes.

This fern has small triangular fronds which grow atop a slender black stem, ranging from 1 to 4 inches in height. As suggested by the common name, a characteristic waxy golden powder, which comes off easily when touched, covers the underside.

California Indians wove black patterns into their baskets by using the goldenback fern stem.

Lady Fern

Fern Family
Polypodiaceae Family

Athyrium filix-femina

Lady fern grows in moist shady areas, usually next to, or very near a water source.

This fern is an annual, sending up new, tightly-curled fronds every year. During late spring and early summer, the small shoots develop into large, 3 to 4 foot long, lacy fronds. These fronds are twice pinnate, which means that the highly-divided pinnae grow off the main stem. Its light green color and deeply fringed pinnae make this fern one of the most beautiful plants in the forest.

Goldenback Fern
Lady Fern

California Maidenhair

Fern Family
Polypodiaceae Family

Adiantum jordanii

California maidenhair is found in moist shaded areas, usually on wet, rocky outcrops. It is fairly rare.

Several erect to gently curving fronds grow out of a single, scaly base. The rounded pinnae grow on small stems which branch off the 1 to 2 foot long central stem. Undercurled margins of the pinnae enclose the spores.

The black stems of the maidenhair were pounded by Indians until they broke into long flat strands, which were woven into baskets as a black pattern. It was the strands of the maidenhair which made the pattern of a special hat called the squaw cap. When a woman was widowed, her hair was burned off at the neckline, then smeared with pine pitch. On top of this, she wore the squaw cap for a year as a sign of her grief.

Western Sword Fern

Fern Family
Polypodiaceae Family

Polystichum munitum

Sword fern grows in shady areas and is commonly found in sheltered canyons in the redwood and mixed evergreen forests.

Like many other ferns, sword fern has several individual fronds arising from a single base. Usually 2 to 4 feet in length, these fronds have blade-like pinnae, arranged alternately along a central stem. At the base of each of these pinna is a small, perpendicular projection. Since this projection resembles the hilt of a sword, it easily identifies this fern. Spores are arranged in round clusters along veins on the underside of the pinnae.

California
Maidenhair

Western
Sword
Fern

Coastal Wood Fern

Dryopteris arguta

The coastal wood fern grows well in the shaded areas found under redwood or mixed evergreen forests.

This is a dark-green perennial fern that grows 8 to 20 inches in height. Growing from a short underground stem, the fronds have slender pinnae which branch off the main axis. These pinnae grow tightly together, giving a ruffled appearance. The sori, which contain the spores, are arranged in 2 rows along the lower surface, and are covered by a horseshoe-shaped flap.

Horsetails

Equisetum species

Horsetails are found along streams or in shaded, boggy locations.

Rising from an extensive underground rootstalk system, the straight, usually unbranched horsetail stems are jointed and hollow between the nodes. Tiny longitudinal grooves run the length of the plant. Leaves, when present, are reduced to toothed sheaths which grow in whorls from the joints. Horsetails are dimorphic, which means that they have both sterile and fertile stems. Like ferns, they reproduce by spores rather than seeds. These spores are borne in terminal structures which resemble small cones.

Horsetails are one of the world's oldest plants and, before evolving into their small present-day form, they covered the earth in giant forests, 50 or more feet tall.

The silicaceous minerals with which horsetails are imbedded are an excellent protection, discouraging most insects and animals from eating them. Livestock sometimes graze on these plants and can be poisoned by them. However, this high mineral content can be useful. There is an old story that miners checked these plants for particles of gold to see if the nearby streams were worth panning. Also, early settlers used the rough plants as a scouring medium.

Coastal Wood Fern

Horsetails

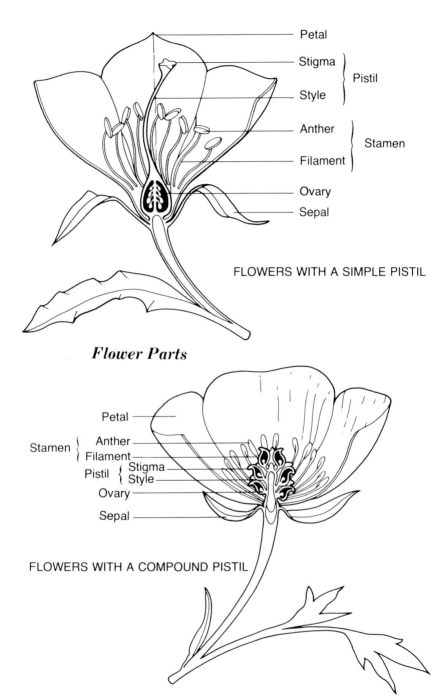

Petal

Stigma
Style
} Pistil

Anther
Filament
} Stamen

Ovary
Sepal

FLOWERS WITH A SIMPLE PISTIL

Flower Parts

Petal

Stamen { Anther
Filament

Pistil { Stigma
Style

Ovary

Sepal

FLOWERS WITH A COMPOUND PISTIL

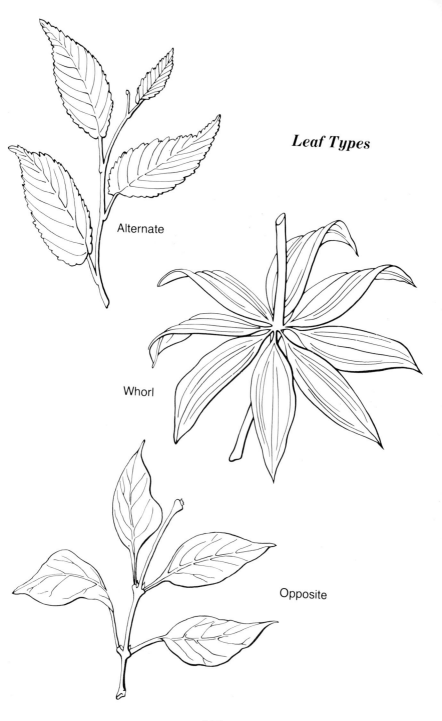

Leaf Types

Alternate

Whorl

Opposite

133

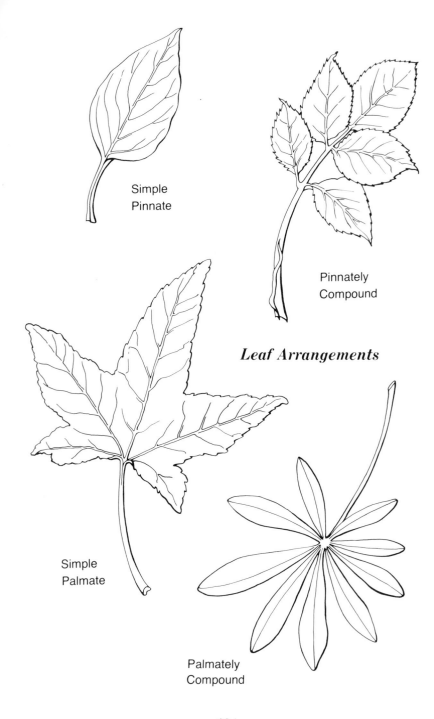

Simple
Pinnate

Pinnately
Compound

Leaf Arrangements

Simple
Palmate

Palmately
Compound

134

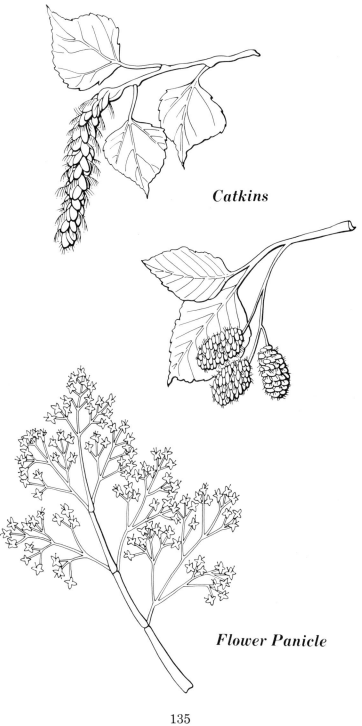

Catkins

Flower Panicle

135

Glossary

Alternate – Leaves situated singly along a stem, arising from different leaf nodes; not in pairs.

Anther – The enlarged part of the stamen that bears pollen.

Basal – Arising from the base of a plant.

Calyx – A collective term for the sepals.

Catkin – A group of flowers, often of one sex, growing tightly-clustered along a stalk.

Compound – A leaf composed of two or more leaflets which look like true leaves.

Corolla – A collective term for petals.

Genus – A universal scientific name for a group of closely related species.

Herbaceous – Plants that do not form woody tissue.

Leaflet – A leaf-like part of a compound leaf.

Lobed – A flower or leaf that has deep indentations.

Node – The place along the stem where leaves arise.

Opposite – Leaves growing along a stem in pairs; arising from the same node.

Palmate – Leaves with 3 or more veins developing from a common center; like a hand.

Perennial – A plant that lives from year to year, including those that die back to bulbs in winter.

Petal – Usually the showy portion of the flower parts; inside the whorl of sepals.

Pinna – (Plural: Pinnae) The leaf-like parts of a fern, often finely divided.

Pinnate – A compound leaf composed of leaflets arranged along a central stalk; featherlike.

Rhizome – A fleshy, underground stem; often called a rootstock.

Saprophyte – A plant that receives nutrients from dead organic matter.

Sepal – The outermost whorl of flower parts, usually green.

Species – A taxonomic term for closely related plants with similar morphological characteristics.

Whorl – Leaves or flower parts that grow from a single location on the stem.

References

Balls, Edward. 1962. *Early Uses of California Plants*. University of California Press, Berkeley.

Clarke, Charlotte Bringle. 1977. *Edible and Useful Plants of California*. University of California Press, Berkeley.

Coon, Nelson. 1969. *Using Wayside Plants*. Hearthside Press, Inc., New York.

Gibbons, Euell. 1974. *Stalking the Wild Asparagus*. David McKay Co., Inc., New York.

Grillos, Steve. 1971. *Ferns and Fern Allies of California*. University of California Press, Berkeley.

Kirk, Donald. R. 1970. *Wild Edible Plants of the Western United States*. Naturegraph Publishers, Healdsburg, Ca.

Merrill, Ruth Earl. 1970. *Plants Used in Basketry by the California Indians*. Acoma Books, Ramona, Ca.

Metcalf, Woodbridge. 1974. *Native Trees of the San Francisco Bay Region*. University of California Press, Berkeley.

Smith, Gladys. 1963. *Flowers and Ferns of Muir Woods*. Muir Woods Natural History Association, Muir Woods National Monument, Ca.

Thomas, John H. 1961. *Flora of the Santa Cruz Mountains of California; A Manual of the Vascular Plants*. Stanford University Press, Stanford, Ca.

Index

141